One and Five Ideas

One and Five Ideas

On Conceptual Art and Conceptualism

TERRY SMITH

EDITED AND WITH AN INTRODUCTION
BY ROBERT BAILEY

DUKE UNIVERSITY PRESS

Durham and London

2017

Interior design by Barbara Wiedemann
Typeset in Chaparral Pro by Copperline

Library of Congress Cataloging-in-Publication Data
Names: Smith, Terry (Terry E.), author. | Bailey, Robert, [date] editor.
Title: One and five ideas : on Conceptual Art and conceptualism /
Terry Smith ; edited and with an introduction by Robert Bailey.
Description: Durham : Duke University Press, 2016. | Includes
bibliographical references and index.
Identifiers:
LCCN 2016016698
ISBN 9780822361121 (hardcover : alk. paper)
ISBN 9780822361312 (pbk. : alk. paper)
ISBN 9780822374329 (e-book)
Subjects: LCSH: Conceptual art. | Conceptualism. | Conceptual
art—Australia. | Conceptual art—New Zealand.
Classification: LCC N6494.C63 S585 2016 | DDC 700—dc23
LC record available at https://lccn.loc.gov/2016016698

Cover art: Joseph Kosuth, *Clock (One and Five)*, 1965. Clock and four works on paper, photograph, and printed paper. Tate Modern, London. Acquisition transferred from the Irish Museum of Modern Art 1997 © Tate, London 2015.

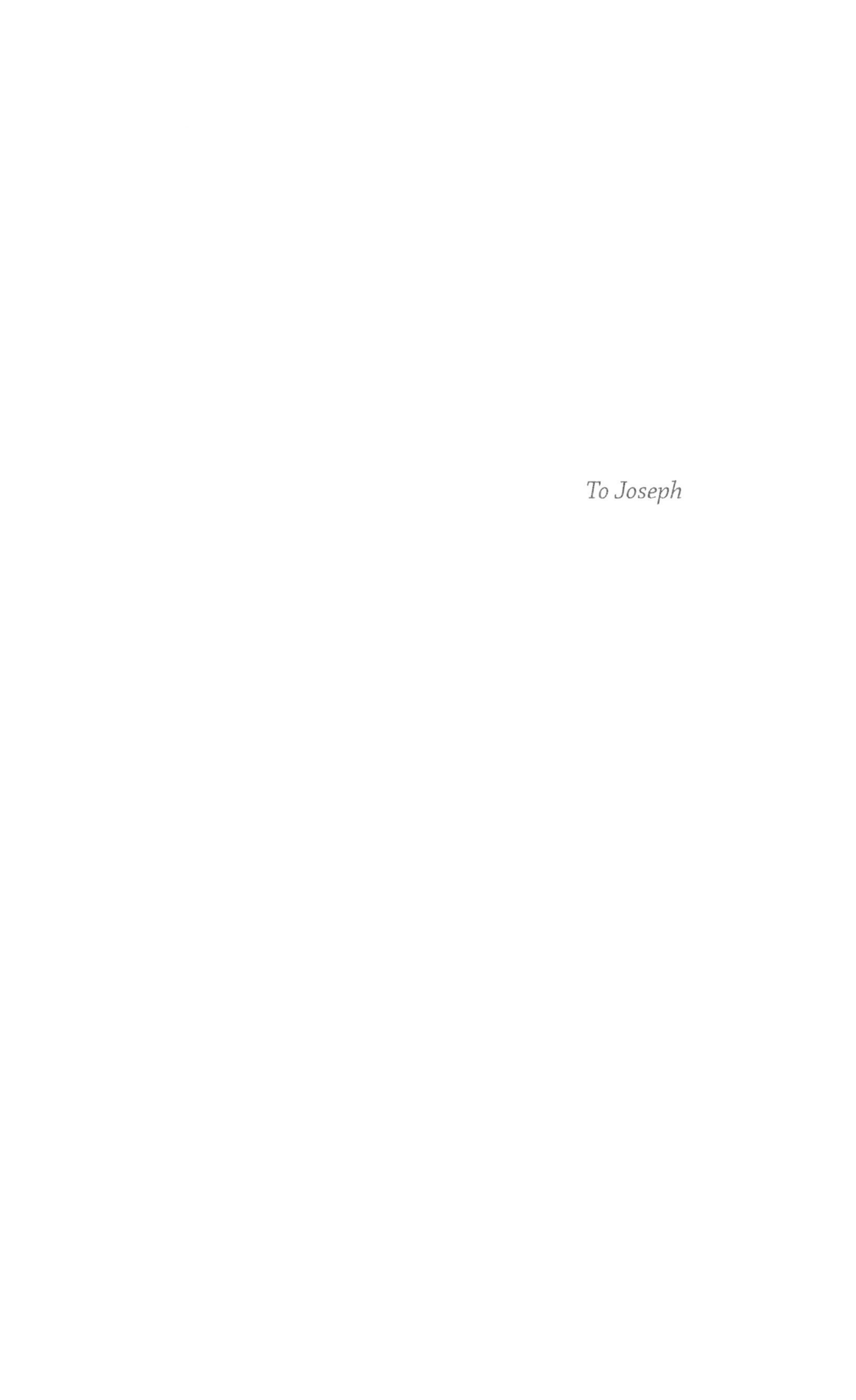

To Joseph

Contents

Illustrations

FIGURES

PLATES *(following page 56)*

Acknowledgments

While it is impossible to acknowledge all of the people across five decades who helped shape these essays at their times of writing, the author would like to specifically acknowledge his gratitude to Ian Burn, Mel Ramsden, Terry Atkinson, Michael Baldwin, and Joseph Kosuth and to the other members of Art & Language with whom he worked in New York, as well as John Coplans, Max Kozloff, and Lawrence Alloway at *Artforum*; John Maynard, Ian Wedde, and Gregory Burke in New Zealand; Mary Kelly, Alexander Alberro, and Blake Stimson; Luis Camnitzer, Jane Farver, and Rachel Weiss in connection with the *Global Conceptualism* exhibition; and Barbara Fisher, Boris Groys, Sarah Wilson, and Anton Vidokle in connection with the genesis of chapter 5. Most of all, he would like to thank this book's editor, for the idea, his work on it, especially the introduction, and for the title.

Both author and editor would like to thank those who have proven essential in the book's coming to be. Joseph Kosuth, Mel Ramsden, Michael Baldwin, Avril Burn, Mary Kelly, and Ray Barrie provided permission to reproduce images. Mary Kelly gave permission to reproduce "A Conversation about Conceptual Art, Subjectivity and the *Post-Partum*

Document," the transcript of a conversation between herself and Terry Smith that took place in Chicago on March 10, 1995. Nadav Hochman provided invaluable assistance with images and permissions, and Ben Ogrodnik provided useful assistance with research. At Duke University Press, Ken Wissoker welcomed the project with great warmth, the outside readers provided crucial critical insight, and Jade Brooks expertly shepherded the book throughout the production process.

All of the texts are reprinted as originally published with only minor modifications, most of which involve the standardization of citations. Original publication information is as follows:

Terry Smith, "Art and Art and Language," *Artforum* 12, no. 6 (February 1974): 49–52.

Terry Smith, "The Tasks of Translation: Art & Language in Australia and New Zealand 1975–76," in Ian Wedde and Gregory Burke, eds., *Now See Hear! Art, Language and Translation* (Wellington, New Zealand: Victoria University Press, 1990), 250–61.

Terry Smith with Mary Kelly, "A Conversation about Conceptual Art, Subjectivity and the *Post-Partum Document*," in Alexander Alberro and Blake Stimson, eds., *Conceptual Art: A Critical Anthology* (Cambridge, MA: MIT Press, 1999), 450–58.

Terry Smith, "Peripheries in Motion: Conceptualism and Conceptual Art in Australia and New Zealand," in Luis Camnitzer, Jane Farver, and Rachel Weiss, eds., *Global Conceptualism: Points of Origin, 1950s–1980s* (New York: Queens Museum of Art, 1999), 87–95.

Terry Smith, "One and Three Ideas: Conceptualism Before, During, and After Conceptual Art," *e-flux journal* 29 (November 2011), http://www.e-flux.com/journal/view/267; subsequently reprinted in Boris Groys, ed., *Moscow Symposium: Conceptualism Revisited* (Berlin: Sternberg, 2012), 42–72.

We thank the many other people and institutions who gave permission to reproduce or reprint images and texts: Art Gallery of South Australia, Adelaide; Generali Foundation, Vienna; Queens Museum Archives, Brooklyn, New York; Zimmerli Art Museum at Rutgers University; Artists Rights Society (ARS), New York; the Renaissance Society at the University of Chicago; Auckland City Art Gallery, Auckland; the

Museum of New Zealand Te Papa, Tongarewa; Art Resource, New York; Art Gallery of Ontario, Toronto; Arts Council Collection, Southbank Centre, London; Mike Parr; Peter Kennedy; Billy Apple; Art Gallery of New South Wales, Sydney; Anna Schwartz Gallery, Sydney; Jim Allen; Govett-Brewster Art Gallery, New Plymouth, New Zealand; Philip Dadson; Museum of Contemporary Art Australia; Leanne Bennett; Woody Ostrow; VAGA Rights, New York; Robert Rauschenberg Foundation; CCCA Canadian Art Database; Society for Reproduction Rights of Authors, Composers and Publishers in Canada (SODRAC), Montreal; the State Tretyakov Gallery, Moscow; Alexander Gray Associates, New York; the Museum of Modern Art, New York; and Tate, London.

Introduction

A Theory of Conceptualism

ROBERT BAILEY

This book brings together Terry Smith's five most important texts about Conceptual Art as a movement and the broader conceptualist tendency in art. Written over five decades, the first in 1974, the most recent in 2012, they amount, in my view, to an important, and distinctive, theory of conceptualism. This theory transcends the contingencies of its occasional presentations to become a set of strong, generalizable claims about what conceptualism is and why it is of the utmost significance for the history of art since the middle of the twentieth century. By yoking its constituent parts together, this introduction aims both to define Smith's theory and to unpack its relationship to the now quite considerable historiography of Conceptual Art and conceptualism. My specific goals are threefold: first, to explicate Smith's theory by identifying its core concerns; second, to show how those concerns relate to the concerns of other scholars; and, finally, to consider the implications of the fact that the theory, in the course of its articulation, came to possess many of the very qualities that it ascribes to the conceptualism for which it accounts.

Smith's work on Conceptual Art and conceptualism is, I want to propose, a dispersed but consistent account that challenges conventional distinctions between artistic practice and scholarly theory. To make this case, I will argue three related claims about it by closely reading Smith's texts and locating them relative both to other scholarship and to the conditions in which they were written. First, I want to suggest that Smith's theory of conceptualism is coherent because it maintains a constant focus on the importance of concepts and, especially, conception for art (and not only for conceptual or conceptualist art). As well, it highlights the capacity for conceptualist art to reconceive the ways in which, at any particular time or in any particular place, art is conceptualized. My second claim is that the discontinuities between the times and places of these texts' authorship, the variety of situations in which they were written, their heterogeneity as to purpose, the ever-changing range of themes they treat, the diversity of formats in which they initially appeared, and the changes over time in Smith's identity as a writer actually assist rather than hinder efforts to comprehend the texts as a unity. In fact, elucidating these differences illuminates the very theory of conceptualism that they articulate, a theory that makes considerable room for the discontinuities that changes in conception inevitably bring about. Indeed, some kind of reconceptualization of Conceptual Art or conceptualism occurs in each of the individual texts and, perhaps even more importantly, in the intervals that elapse between them. Hence my third claim: that Smith's texts perform the very reconceiving of art that they posit as conceptualist art's main purpose, and they are thus, by their own criteria, conceptualist texts that have ramifications concerning what the concept of art is understood to be as well as how art and writing about art are both taken to conceive of that concept.

CONCEPTION AND RECONCEIVING

The five texts that Smith dedicates to Conceptual Art and conceptualism—four essays and one transcribed conversation—each appeared under circumstances that affect the accounts he gives. Each of them was also shaped to varying degrees by his direct involvement in the Conceptual Art collective Art & Language, an involvement that spanned 1972 to 1976. These are the years in which Smith developed the ideas about Conceptual Art that have, over time, gradually become his theory of conceptualism, and they arose in close rapport with that for which they account. Art & Language had coalesced during the mid-1960s at Coventry College of Art in England.[1] Taking as its impetus the idea of using language as a primary means for making visual art, in 1969, it added a like-minded New York contingent that Smith subsequently joined while living in the city as both a student of art history and an aspiring art critic.[2] Art & Language still exists today, despite a tumultuous history that culminated in 1976 with a major purge of membership, including the entirety of its New York section and Smith, by then returned to his native Australia, along with it. During his time with Art & Language,

Smith worked closely with a group of artists and critics who, under the collective's name, were among the earliest practitioners of Conceptual Art, and this provided him with valuable firsthand insight into Conceptual Art as a participant-observer.[3] He took part in making the collective's highly intellectual and conceptually rigorous work, which emerged from its discussions about art and, during the period of Smith's involvement, appeared mostly as texts published in journals or as installations called indexes that drew on linguistics, information theory, computing, and the philosophies of language and science to organize the work that Art & Language was doing into complex, recursive structures resembling library catalog systems and hypertext.

Smith became involved with Art & Language primarily because of his earlier work as an art critic. He had written in that capacity since 1968 for the national newspapers of Australia as well as a variety of national and international art magazines. He was also involved in founding the journal *Other Voices* in 1970, for which he wrote one of his first lengthy pieces, "Color-Form Painting: Sydney 1967–1970," which assayed the latest developments in modernist painting in Australia.[4] In 1972, he received the prestigious Harkness Fellowship, which enabled him to study at New York University and Columbia University in New York. Upon arrival, he connected with two participants in Art & Language: the artists Ian Burn (himself Australian) and Mel Ramsden (who had attended school in Australia along with Burn). Smith had previously included their work in an exhibition entitled *The Situation Now: Object or Post-Object Art?*, which he co-curated with Tony McGillick in 1971 at the Contemporary Art Society of Australia in Sydney.[5] This exhibition, which drew on the critic Donald Brook's concept of "post-object art," was among the very first exhibitions to feature Conceptual Art in Australia.

Smith's interest in Conceptual Art became more pronounced after his arrival in New York and his participation in Art & Language began. In tracking the development of his thinking about Conceptual Art and, later, conceptualism from these early origins to its culmination decades later, I want to begin by briefly outlining the basic circumstances in which each of Smith's texts was written so as to identify their major points of commonality. Following that, I will devote the main part of this introduction to a critical exposition of how his theory of conceptualism evolves and takes shape over the course of its development.

"Art and Art and Language," Smith's first substantial account of Conceptual Art, appeared in the February 1974 issue of *Artforum*.[6] This essay considers Art & Language's work in relation to the current state of thinking about art. Ideas that become, and remain, central to his thinking on Conceptual Art appear in it for the first time, particularly his interest in what "conception" means in the context of the visual arts.[7] Specifically, Smith tries to show how certain widely held conceptions of art current in the art world at the time were unable to comprehend Art & Language's work. The essay was, like all work done by Art & Language at this time, circulated within the collective and commented on by it prior to publication, and it owes a considerable amount to the intellectual atmosphere then prevailing in the group, especially the collective's interest in the philosophy of science. As Smith notes in "Art and Art and Language," alluding to Thomas S. Kuhn and his influential theories of paradigms and paradigm shifts, "It became clear to me that the making of art entailed the holding of a set of theories about art (to which T. S. Kuhn's notion of paradigm seems only an approximate analogy), theory-sets constituted by notions of what the world is like."[8] Kuhn defined a paradigm as a consensus composed of intertwining theoretical commitments and professional practices collectively and conventionally adhered to by scientists in order to pursue the acquisition of knowledge.[9] Though Smith puts some distance between this concept and his own "theory-sets," the two notions partake of a basic idea that a body of theoretical commitments has fundamental entailments for practical activity in the world, and such an idea, tied to the concept of a conception, remains a part of Smith's theory across the entire course of its development.

Over a decade would pass before Smith again wrote about Conceptual Art in as substantive a way as he had in "Art and Art and Language." In 1990, he published an essay entitled "The Tasks of Translation: Art & Language in Australia & New Zealand 1975–6" for a catalog accompanying *Now See Hear! Art, Language and Translation*, an exhibition at the Wellington City Art Gallery in Wellington, New Zealand. This essay discusses the role of translation in a number of Art & Language exhibitions focused on provincialism and the geopolitics of art worlds that Smith organized in Melbourne, Adelaide, and Auckland during 1975 and 1976.[10] For each of these shows, a comprehensive selection of Art & Language's work, nearly all of it made in England and New York, was presented in Australia and New Zealand, and Smith, himself the only person involved in Art & Language who was present at the exhibitions, facilitated discussions modeled after Art & Language's own with invited guests and interested audiences. These conversations took as their points of departure the work being shown in the exhibitions and the implications of its traveling from places perceived as centers to places perceived as peripheries with the aim of contesting provincial attitudes and their attendant conceptions of art.[11] In "The Tasks of Translation," Smith puts forward the ideas that conceptual artists such as himself pursued "the possibility of radically reconceiving art altogether" and that the role of translator that Smith assumed by mediating between Art & Language's work and its audiences might be one way of enacting such a reconceptualization of art.[12] Here, the idea of reconceiving, which was already implicit in the hostile way that Smith treated certain conceptions of art while advocating for Art & Language's own in "Art and Art and Language," becomes an explicit and forceful part of his thinking moving forward. Along with conception, reconceiving would become the other centerpiece of Smith's theory, which the subsequent essays would continue to extrapolate.

A 1995 conversation between Smith, speaking again as a former member of Art & Language, and the artist Mary Kelly appeared in 1999 under the title "A Conversation about Conceptual Art, Subjectivity and the *Post-Partum Document*."[13] This conversation, which includes Smith's next major statement about Conceptual Art, further unpacks how the intensely analytic "work on the concept of art" that Art & Language did in the early 1970s—the kind he wrote about in "Art and Art and Language"—occasioned a transformation in the collective's own conception of art that enabled the social and political work it did later on during his tenure with the group, including in the exhibitions he discusses in "The Tasks of Translation."[14] Smith's deepening recognition of a political turn in Conceptual Art that emerges from the art's capacity to reconceive art—an idea that gets developed largely through conversation with Kelly, who espouses her own important ideas about Conceptual Art's politics, which are tied largely to feminism—proves to be a key component of Smith's subsequent work on conceptualism. This new emphasis on politics also shows Smith's own thinking on Conceptual Art undergoing a reconceptualization as his understanding of the movement changes.

A similar reassessment, this time with respect to geography rather than politics, marks Smith's turn from thinking about Conceptual Art to thinking about conceptualism, which begins in 1999 with his curatorial contribution to *Global Conceptualism: Points of Origin 1950s–1980s*. This exhibition transformed how Conceptual Art and conceptualism are discussed by making a case for the worldwide appearance of a broad and politically radical "attitudinal expression" in art called conceptualism that starts to emerge around the midpoint of the twentieth century.[15] Whether or not it includes the familiar and largely North American and

Western European Conceptual Art movement is a matter of debate, but not up for debate is any notion that conceptualism is reducible to the prerogatives of Conceptual Art. On the contrary, *Global Conceptualism* focused intensely on local concerns. The globe was divided into eleven regions, with a local curator responsible for each one. Smith's section showed his selection of artists from Australia and New Zealand. His accompanying catalog essay, "Peripheries in Motion: Conceptualism and Conceptual Art in Australia and New Zealand," puts forward an argument about the salience of geographical mobility to the emergence, development, and legacy of conceptualism in Australia and New Zealand, as artists and critics, including a few (such as himself) involved with Art & Language, relocated from what they perceived to be peripheral and provincial southern cities to the capitals of the northern hemisphere to pursue "a conceptual questioning of the nature of art."[16] Smith again makes much of conceptualism's capacity to reconceive the concept of art, and he places this idea at the forefront of his account of the geographies of conceptualism in (and out of) Australia and New Zealand as artists were exposed, through travel, to new ideas about art.

Smith's effort to develop his thinking about Conceptual Art into a more generally applicable theory of conceptualism finds its fullest expression in the latest and most comprehensive statement of his position, which derives from an art-historical perspective inflected by his deep interest in the contemporaneity of contemporary art.[17] This essay, entitled "One and Three Ideas: Conceptualism Before, During, and After Conceptual Art," first appeared in print in connection with a symposium organized in Moscow by Boris Groys during 2011 to reconsider the emergence of conceptualism in the Soviet Union by situating it relative to international contexts.[18] Smith's text puts forward the idea that conceptualisms, whether the Conceptual Art in which he was involved as a participant in Art & Language or the sort of art that Groys wrote about at an early date in Moscow, adhere to different "conceptions of conceptualism" that each partake, by reconceiving various local artistic traditions, in a more comprehensive pursuit of the mutual recognition that conceptual thinking affords.[19] Achieving this mutual recognition resulted in conceptualism playing a crucial role in the emergence of a global contemporary art. In this final iteration, Smith's theory provides a comprehensive assessment of conceptualism centered on its geopolitics of conception and reconceiving art and its historical importance for the emergence of contemporary art.

FROM THE CONCEPT OF ART TO CONCEPTUALISM

The broad spans of time separating these five very different occasions and the diverse roles—critic, theorist, artist, curator, and art historian—that Smith played while partaking of them have yielded a theory of conceptualism that is both wide in its implications for the understanding of conceptualism in art and yet also precise in its focus on how artists conceptualize and reconceive art's being and doing. My first pass through Smith's five texts prioritized the theoretical continuity within them. It is, however, just as important to explore the differences between these texts and between the occasions of their authorship, as these differences have a significant bearing on the theory that Smith articulates and the way he articulates it. They provide it with nuance, scope, and qualifications alike. Indeed, each time Smith writes or speaks of Conceptual Art or conceptualism, he is writing at a different time, in a different place, in a different role, with different collaborators and interlocutors, with different concerns, and in an altogether different genre of writing or mode of discourse. These differences demand at least as much attention as the theory's main argumentation concerning the geopolitics of reconceiving conceptions of art and their historical salience for subsequent art. Moreover, these differences also enable Smith's theory to be situated much more clearly vis-à-vis the contexts of Conceptual Art, conceptualism, their historiographies, and the wider histories within which all of these developments take place.

The history of writing about Conceptual Art begins during the late 1960s before Smith's involvement in it. The movement itself came of age during a period marked by political upheaval and activist politics as well as equally radical developments in intellectual history: structuralism and poststructuralism; new approaches to Marxist theory and psychoanalysis; major changes in the philosophy of language and the philosophy of science; and the consolidation of entirely new fields, including information theory, communication theory, systems theory, cybernetics, and computing.[20] In a sense, Conceptual Art was the artistic equivalent of these developments, equally radical in ambition and transformative in practice, and it drew much from interdisciplinary borrowings or parallels to other kinds of thought and activity. Widespread recognition of this new artistic movement coalescing in New York and elsewhere prompted a number of the artists, critics, and curators involved with it to propose theories about it. Each thinker endeavored to account for art that, at the time, appeared altogether new and strange in its rejection of any number of traditional artistic emphases. Three approaches—those of Lucy Lippard, Sol LeWitt, and Joseph Kosuth—proved to offer the most enduring and influential accounts of this art, despite deriving from radically diverse insights about the reason for calling it "Conceptual Art." Lippard elucidated what she and John Chandler, in a coauthored essay that appeared in *Art International* in February 1968, called "the dematerialization of art."[21] While discussing "ultra-conceptual" art, they raise the possibility of "the object's becoming wholly obsolete" as art becomes increasingly focused on conceptual matters.[22] LeWitt, meanwhile, in texts from 1967 and 1969, also pointed to the waning importance of the art object. For him, "the idea [or] concept is the most important aspect" of a conceptual artwork, and he reduced the actual making of the object to "a perfunctory affair."[23] Though LeWitt proposed that "ideas alone can be works of art" and "all ideas need not be made physical," his own ideas, like his concepts, still tended toward the object—that is, whether "made physical" or not, they were ideas or concepts that were meant to be realized as material objects, even if the bulk of an artist's effort was transposed toward the realm of ideating and conceptualizing.[24]

Operating at a remove from both Lippard's idealistic vision of concepts replacing objects and LeWitt's emphasis on the rather teleological role that concepts play in the making of objects, Kosuth aligned Conceptual Art closely with philosophy and considered it to be an "inquiry into the foundations of the concept 'art,' as it has come to mean."[25] Here, the focus of Conceptual Art is placed squarely on a concept—"art"—and on an artistic investigation of that concept.[26] Material, formal, and aesthetic concerns do not vanish so much as they come to serve conceptual considerations. Indeed, for Kosuth, the value of an artist "can be weighed according to how much they questioned the nature of art; which is another way of saying 'what they *added* to the conception of art' or what wasn't there before they started."[27] Kosuth even goes so far as to distinguish his own "'purest' definition of conceptual art" from "'conceptual art' . . . considered as a *tendency*," an idea later taken up and developed by those who have sought to identify and name internal differentiations within the category of Conceptual Art as well as by those who, even later, began distinguishing a geographically and chronologically specific Conceptual Art movement from a more open and diffuse conceptualist tendency.[28] In such accounts, the Art & Language group often figure as exemplary practitioners of Conceptual Art at its "purest,"

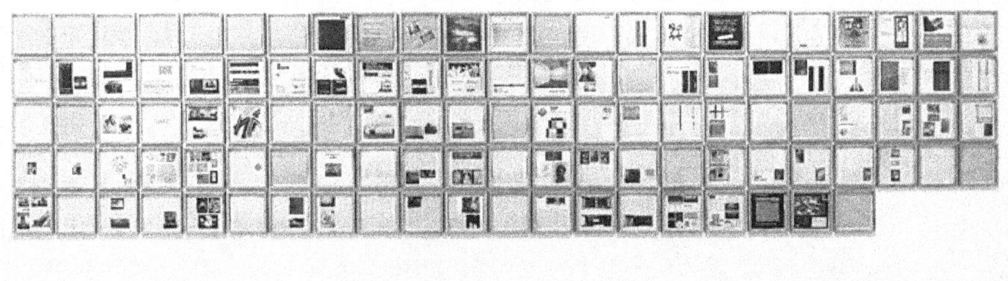

Art & Language, Comparative Models, *1972, installation view.*

much to the chagrin of those who prefer a less rigid understanding of these things.[29]

Smith's "Art and Art and Language" appeared at the tail end of this initial reception and had the benefit of some hindsight as a result. The movement's significance—and with it Art & Language's—had recently been assured through major exhibitions, including *When Attitudes Become Form* (1969), *Information* (1970), and *Documenta 5* (1972), that provided Conceptual Art with mainstream institutional recognition from the museums and biennials that were increasingly its sources. This was consolidated by the appearance of the first books about the movement, anthologies edited by Ursula Meyer (1972), Lippard (1973), and Gregory Battcock (1973) that confirmed widespread interest in Conceptual Art.[30] Although each of these exhibitions and books configured Conceptual Art differently and staked different claims about it, they converge in a shared acknowledgment that this new kind of art was a phenomenon of major importance. Smith's essay responds to this emerging consensus by defending Art & Language's work against the way it was being received in venues such as these legitimating exhibitions and books. Believing, as the collective had come to do, that none of the available claims about Conceptual Art had much purchase on its work (excepting that of Kosuth, who was by this time himself a participant in Art & Language), Smith announces, "A&L is different not just in degree but in kind from its 'Conceptual art' origins."[31] Staking such a claim before 1972 would have been typical of early efforts like Lippard's, LeWitt's, and Kosuth's to identify more precisely what Conceptual Art is and is not, but after the initial wave of critical and curatorial interest in the movement, this kind of claim indicates a shift in thinking about Conceptual Art toward an acknowledgment of its becoming a historical phenomenon that could now be contested as such. Smith's essay is thus an early manifestation of a turn in how Conceptual Art would subsequently be discussed, namely, as art history. As one of the first writings about Conceptual Art to encounter it as a phenomenon capable of being discussed not only through retrospection but also through a retrospection that could argue with other competing retrospections, it is also one of the first texts on Conceptual Art to pursue a deliberately heterodox take on the movement.

Revealing an inclination toward Kosuth's thinking about Conceptual Art, particularly his interest in the concept of art and the role conceptions of it come to play, in "Art and Art and Language," Smith laments the "fundamental conceptions of what it is to make art, to be an artist, and to understand art" within the art world as of 1974.[32] "It seemed imperative to determine what these conceptions were, how they related to one another, how they functioned in other contexts, and how they so thoroughly informed the making of art."[33] Conceptions receive their first definition here as that which positions the thinking and doing from which art emerges and is received.[34] The body of Smith's essay is devoted to spelling out what the available conceptions in the art world were at the time and how their limitations foreclose a sufficient reckoning with what Art & Language's "point of view" offers in their stead.[35] The idea that art is entangled with conceptions is not entirely new here—Kosuth stated that "all art is finally conceptual" as early as 1969—but Smith's definition of conceptions involves much more than the concept of art.[36] He includes under the heading of a conception not only the meaning of "art" but also an entire domain of activities conducted in the vicinity of art—producing artworks, socializing as an artist, interpreting works of art, comparing theories, and so on—that follow from how art is conceived. Art does not only add (or not add) something to the available ways of conceptualizing art by questioning the concept of art, as it does for Kosuth; it is now understood to operate fully in accordance with a conception of what art is that has come to be one of art's conditions of possibility. "The key cause of art's misfortune," Smith contends, speaking here about the available conceptions of art, "is that, through the past decade, each one of these theory-sets, having initially clustered together to form open concepts of art for those who employed them, have become progressively more closed, fixed, overdetermined through continual usage and ever more refined self-definition. They no longer have the generative power of 'essentially contested concepts': all too clear criteria for their 'proper' use has been developed."[37] Speaking more directly to Art & Language's project, which "reveal[s] a critique of this sort," he suggests that its refusal of "the instincts and practices of mid-'60s Conceptual art" preceded the development of "a distinctively A&L set of intentions" that jettisoned an ossifying notion of Conceptual Art in pursuit of new ways to vivify artistic practice.[38]

This may seem like an exciting time for Conceptual Art, but it was actually flagging, and interest in it falls off after the mid-1970s. Such interest does not pick up again until the late 1980s when a flurry of activity—largely mediated through retrospective exhibitions at European (and, a few years later, American) museums—revived it at a time when a resurgent art market had prompted a conservative return to traditional mediums in art. In light of this, Conceptual Art appeared important again as an alternative to the glut of expressionist paintings and slick sculptures filling up art galleries because it was the major predecessor to the more critical practices then contesting these developments. In particular, Benjamin H. D. Buchloh's and Charles Harrison's contributions to the catalogs of the earliest Conceptual Art retrospectives, especially the 1989 exhibition *L'art conceptuel, une perspective* at the Musée d'Art Moderne de la Ville de Paris, established the movement's enduring art-historical significance by emphasizing its challenges to the presumption, maintained in the West since the onset of modernity, of art's essentially visual nature and the related tendency to regard engagement with art entirely in terms of beholding.[39] Buchloh's equation of Conceptual Art with an "elimination of visuality and traditional definitions of representation" and Harrison's claim for its "suppression of the disinterested spectator" positioned Conceptual Art as a definitive rupture with artistic modernism and its preoccupation with the optical and the aesthetic, precisely what recent painting and sculpture were endeavoring to reclaim in spectacular fashion during the 1980s.[40] Buchloh's account also began to situate Conceptual Art more deeply within its social, political, and economic contexts, which he took to be "the operating logic of late capitalism."[41] This led to the idea that Conceptual Art begat a sequel of sorts in a movement called institutional critique, something much explored by scholars and artists since, which took a critical look at how museums, markets, and the social institution of art function and, in so doing, provided a leftist alternative to the neoliberalism then in rapid ascendency in the art world as elsewhere.[42]

While Smith was not involved directly in these exhibitions, his es-

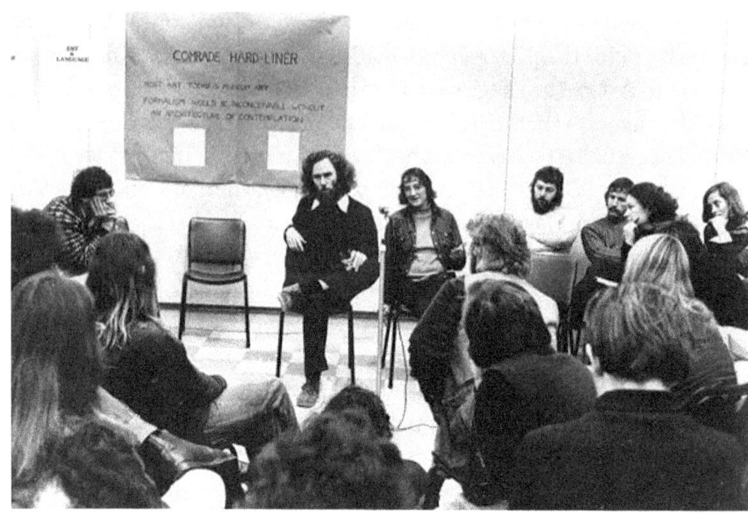

Art & Language, Art & Language, *1975, Art Gallery of South Australia, Adelaide (Terry Smith and Lucy Lippard).*

say "The Tasks of Translation" is contemporaneous with them and partakes of their retrospective validation of Conceptual Art, including its contestation of institutional power, as an important part of recent art history, albeit in different ways. Following an introduction that asserts the thesis that "the demands of the mid-1970s moment created a new role for certain artists, and for newly empowered art audiences: that of *translator*," the essay includes theoretical considerations of translation that draw on the writings of Walter Benjamin and Jacques Derrida, an assessment of the salience of translation for Conceptual Art in general, and then one section each covering Smith's 1975 Australian exhibitions and 1976 New Zealand exhibition as a member of Art & Language, both of which are discussed as instances of translation. The second section on Conceptual Art announces that, in the 1960s and 1970s, "the concept of Art was up for grabs" and further shows how the linguistic and theoretical emphases of Conceptual Art enabled Art & Language to confront the geographical disparities of globalizing art worlds by making translation and communication into a means for reconceiving art.[43]

Smith's account of translation was not particularly impressive to its first respondent, who accused him of being forgetful on at least two counts. Ian Burn, himself a participant in Art & Language's work during the period in question, also contributed a text to the volume in which "The Tasks of Translation" originally appeared. It includes a brief note in which Burn voices his dissatisfaction with the way Smith frames Art & Language's work of the mid-1970s. "For the record," he writes, "I take issue with much of Terry Smith's account (published elsewhere in this book) of the 1960s and 70s which he offers as a background to the Art & Language 'exhibitions' in Australia in 1975 and New Zealand in 1976."[44] Burn states that Smith "fails to refer" to the "considerable history" of interest in translation in both art and intellectual life prior to his involvement with Art & Language. He has in mind, among other things, his own work on translation, which drew on "a wide range of sources, from John Cage and Jasper Johns to Wittgenstein, Barthes and further."[45] Burn is correct that the work *Soft-Tape*, which he developed together with Mel Ramsden in 1966, predates Smith's exhibitions by roughly a decade, and he is also correct that many of the ideas about translation advanced in it provide highly germane background to the Art & Language work that Smith did in Australia and New Zealand.[46]

Smith would fully register the precedent of *Soft-Tape*, an audio piece in which a recorded voice gets played back at such low volume that the words it recites are nearly inaudible, by featuring it prominently in *Global Conceptualism* and discussing it in detail in his catalog essay for that exhibition.[47] However, his early glossing of it would not likely have met with Burn's ire had it not led, in his mind, to something else: a misconception. Burn's more enduring and open-ended criticism of "The Tasks of Translation" is his claim that, "in Terry's essay, the concerns of Art & Language are represented as narrow and singular, involved in 'obsessive self-examination.' This he 'proves' by suppressing reference to the disparate range of work being done. Violent disagreements and conflicts abounded about the priorities of various kinds of work and, at any one time, there were always competing streams of activity."[48] Burn is especially suspicious of Smith's claims that he functioned as a translator during Art & Language's 1975 exhibitions in Australia. "Regarding that show," he says, "the point—as Mel [Ramsden] and I saw it then—was never that a new role 'of translator' was being proposed for artists."[49] Instead, Burn suggests, the purpose of these exhibitions was, through Smith's mediation, to produce "noise" rather than the comprehension that a translator is tasked with producing.[50]

Although Burn's note is concerned only with this one text of Smith's, it has wider ramifications for the theory of conceptualism that developed in large part out of its declared interest in reconceiving art. By accusing Smith of propagating a misconception about Art & Language, he raises a number of issues about conceptions and reconceiving, particularly where the matter of error arises. In 1974, Smith had lauded Art & Language for being "complex and many-sided" as well as "subject to change—constantly on surface levels, occasionally in radical depth."[51] He even goes as far as staking a claim to the effect that "part of the dynamic of the group depends on the diversity of outlook of its members" and thus that what Burn calls "disagreements and conflicts" are constitutive for its way of working.[52] Smith himself opposed this diversity of thought to the various "*mis*conceptions" of Art & Language work that he itemizes in "Art and Art and Language" under the headings "*A&L is visual art in the forms of writing/words/text/book*," "*The 'art' in A&L writings lies in the style in which they are written*," "*A&L in relation to philosophy*," and "*A&L as a form of Conceptual Art*," each of which he criticizes, among other things, for being overly reductive.[53]

Roughly a decade and a half later, Burn accuses Smith of making this same mistake and trafficking in an incomplete, reductive, or otherwise badly formulated conception of Art & Language's activity. The conception of the conceptual artist as a translator that he finds in Smith's text is one that leaves out the anarchic character of Art & Language's discussions and prioritizes translation's capacity to operate between incommensurable languages, ways of thinking, or localities over the difficulties thereof that Art & Language would have been prioritizing at the time in question.[54] All of this matters at the wider level of Smith's theory of conceptualism because it points to its lack of explicit criteria both for identifying what constitutes a well-formulated conception and for distinguishing between a beneficial and a detrimental reconceptualization.[55] These are, of course, complicated matters. No resolution to the problems they pose, easy or otherwise, is likely to be found by accounting for Conceptual Art, and it would be an understatement to say that there is no consensus among epistemologists or philosophers of mind where such things are concerned. Nevertheless, Burn suggests important and cautious provisos that are worth bearing in mind.

In making these criticisms, Burn also kept open the question of how Art & Language and, by extension, Conceptual Art are best understood and thus partook, along with Smith himself, in a revisionist movement that arose immediately antecedent to the earliest retrospectives of Conceptual Art.[56] Following the consensus-building efforts of these exhibitions, many other voices posed claims about the movement's historical significance by revising, rejecting, or displacing the positions about it staked out by their curators and catalog essayists. This launched the first of what became several waves of revisionism in the 1990s and 2000s focused on a diverse range of topics.[57] Two in particular have unsettled some basic assumptions about Conceptual Art that have affected the way Art & Language and, with it, Smith's work on Conceptual Art get valued. A growing interest in conceptual artists' uses of photography has disproven the idea that Conceptual Art is necessarily hostile to the visual.[58] Similarly, an interest in what is sometimes called "romantic conceptualism" has drawn attention to emotional and affective elements in art that is usually taken to be cerebral and calculating.[59] In both cases, Art & Language proved to be beyond the pale of interest. This compounded reservations about its approach voiced earlier amid Conceptual Art's initial wave of retrospective attention. Buchloh, for instance, had lambasted what he perceived as Art & Language's "authoritarian quests for orthodoxy."[60] Even Harrison, himself a participant in Art & Language and a longtime editor of its journal *Art-Language*, lamented that "Art & Language could identify no *actual* alternative public which was not composed of the participants in its own projects and deliberations."[61]

Eventually, however, this retrospection and revisionism would begin to revise and rehabilitate Art & Language. Ten years after Buchloh's and Harrison's criticisms, "A Conversation about Conceptual Art, Subjectivity and the *Post-Partum Document*" first appeared alongside a number of other texts by or about Art & Language and its former members in Alexander Alberro and Blake Stimson's influential anthology *Conceptual Art: A Critical Anthology*, which strongly reasserts the collective's value for understanding Conceptual Art. The conversation between Smith and Kelly took place in Chicago while Smith was both a visiting professor in the Department of Art History at the University of Chicago and the director of the Public Spheres and the Globalization of Media program, housed within the university's Humanities Institute (now the Franke Institute for the Humanities) and directed by the cultural anthropologist Arjun Appadurai at the time. It was in the latter capacity that Smith made plans to invite a number of key figures in the Conceptual Art movement, including Kelly, Kosuth, Allan Sekula, and Hans Haacke, to come to Chicago for discussions about their work and its ties to Conceptual Art. Only the Kelly discussion, which occurred over two days, has appeared in print to date.[62]

Ostensibly about Kelly's landmark work *Post-Partum Document*, an installation that documents her son's acquisition of language and that

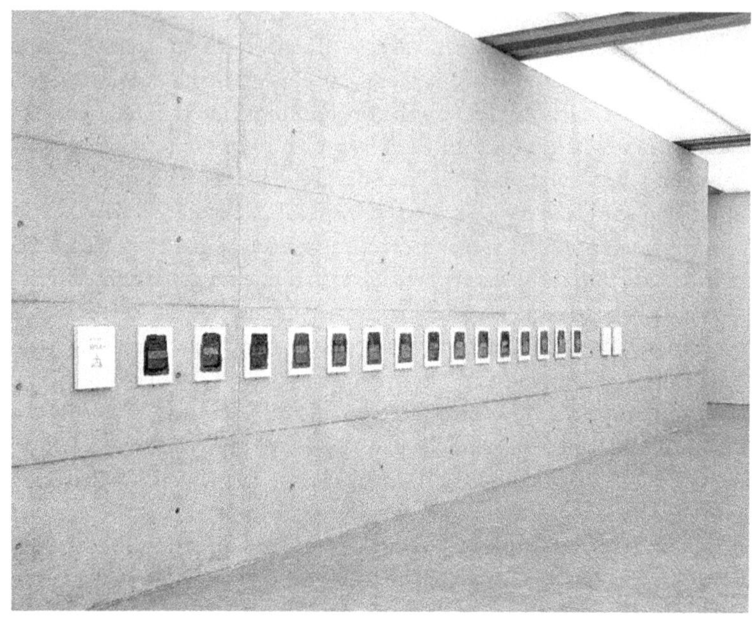

Exhibition view, Mary Kelly. Post-Partum Document. The Complete Work (1973–79), *Generali Foundation, Vienna, 1998, showing* Documentation VI: Pre-Writing Alphabet, Exergue and Diary / Experimentum Mentis VI: (On the Insistence of the Letter), *1978–79.* *© Generali Foundation Collection. Photo: Werner Kaligofsky.*

incorporates psychoanalytic and feminist themes into Conceptual Art, the first part of the discussion between Smith and Kelly ranges widely over topics including subjectivity, gender, power, politics, and their intersections with one another in Conceptual Art, further extrapolating the social, economic, and political contextualization of Conceptual Art begun in earnest by Buchloh.[63] Echoing "Art and Art and Language," Smith speaks about the earlier "propositional" practices of Art & Language, and he focuses on how the group's practice came to center on and develop "work on the concept of art."[64] For Art & Language, what had begun as analytic work became "synthetic" when it turned, around 1974 or 1975, toward "subjects and experiences which were much broader than art and its languages."[65] Indeed, Art & Language began collaborating with a number of far left activist collectives then assembling in New York to confront sexism and racism in the art world and in society more generally, including Artists Meeting for Cultural Change and the Congress of Afrikan Peoples. Furthermore, Smith, having returned to Australia in 1975, had organized the Art & Language exhibitions both there and in New Zealand that he discusses in "The Tasks of Translation."[66] All of this work paralleled Kelly's own developing political interests, which were much wider in scope than those usually held within the Western Conceptual Art movement. Anticipating his subsequent work on conceptualism, Smith notes that art's turn toward the political occurred "all over the world . . . sometimes earlier, sometimes later."[67]

Throughout the conversation, Kelly's voice and *Post-Partum Document* provide a counterpoint to Smith's thinking about Art & Language's work as it moved from an intensely propositional and analytic practice toward a more broadly social and political endeavor. The conversation reiterates Smith's commitment to the idea, which he first broached in "Art and Art and Language," that the history of Conceptual Art involves phases or stages of development in which its conceptuality gets reconfigured. Both Kelly and Smith are in agreement that Conceptual Art includes within it a moment in which art took an important turn toward theoretically sophisticated politics, but she points to certain limitations in Art & Language's inadequate engagement with individual subjectivity, which she claims to emerge from its aversion to integrating psychoanalytic thinking about the personal with its Marxist outlook toward the social, something Kelly made a key part of her own work. Indeed, it was a psychoanalytic, specifically Lacanian, understanding of language's role in subject formation, coupled with a feminist interest in motherhood and women's labor, that motivated Kelly to produce *Post-Partum Document*, and Kelly and Smith discuss that work in part by comparing it to Art & Language's well-known *Index 01* of 1972. The latter work is the culminating statement of Art & Language's initial "propositional" period, and as such it provided Kelly's *Post-Partum Document* with a model to which it reacted by opening the intensity and meticulousness of conceptual investigation in art onto more political concerns, as Art & Language was itself doing around the same time.

FROM CONCEPTUALISM TO CONTEMPORARY ART

The most consequential pivot in the revision of Conceptual Art's history following the initial wave of retrospectives in the late 1980s and revisionism of the 1990s has gradually proven to be a curatorial effort led by Luis Camnitzer, Jane Farver, and Rachel Weiss, who organized the

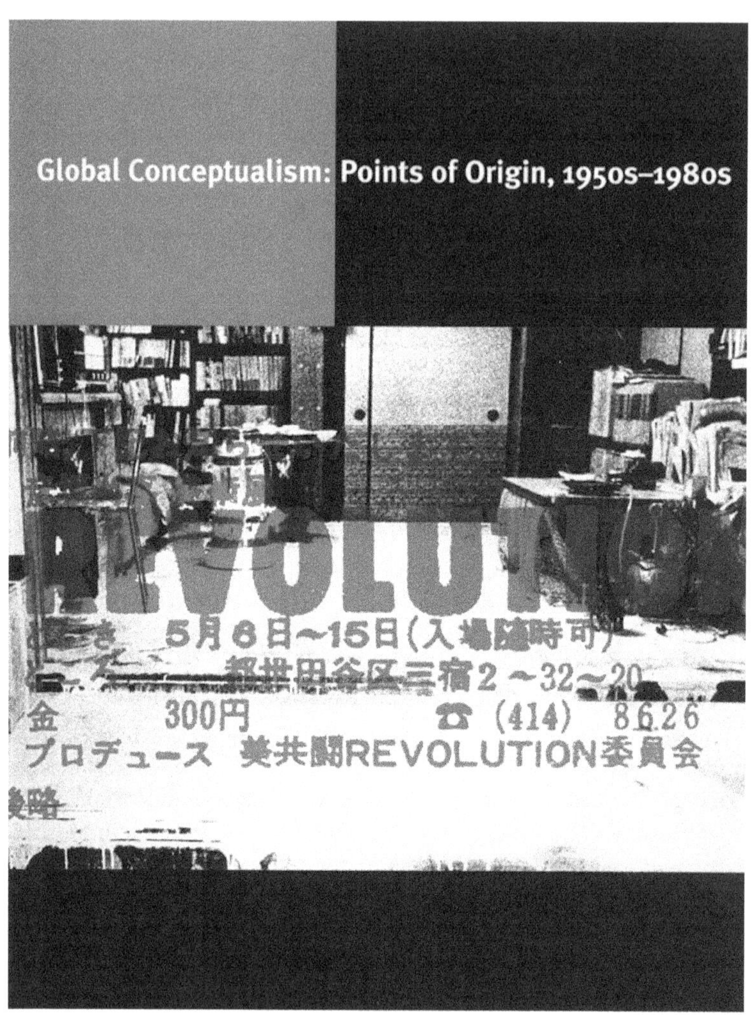

Global Conceptualism: Points of Origin, 1950s–1980s.
Catalog cover of exhibition at Queens Museum of Art, New York, 1999.
Courtesy of the Queens Museum Archives.

Global Conceptualism exhibition in 1999 that inaugurated a large-scale reconceptualization of what is at stake historically in art's turn to the conceptual. The exhibition involved curators from around the world, who together asserted a many-voiced claim that the Conceptual Art movement that Lippard, LeWitt, Kosuth, Buchloh, Harrison, and others discussed was perhaps but one component of a much more widely adopted tendency in postwar art called conceptualism. Ten years after the end of the Cold War and a subsequent rearrangement of world affairs, the consolidation of globalized art institutions such as biennial exhibitions, franchised museums, and international markets—themselves part of globalization's broader cultural, social, and economic impact—would seem to have necessitated a search for the origins of an art capable of contesting these institutions and historical forces at the global scale of their new reign. Conceptualism came together for these curators as an artistic tendency that itself arose globally at, as they proposed, distinct "points of origin," from which it contested local forms of these newly emergent modes of world power.

To recover the unity of this dispersed art, *Global Conceptualism*'s organizers demarcated a hard and fast difference between the by-then familiar Western Conceptual Art movement and a globally emergent conceptualism in their foreword to the exhibition catalog:

> It is important to delineate a clear distinction between *conceptual art* as a term used to denote an essentially formalist practice developed in the wake of minimalism, and *conceptualism*, which broke decisively from the historical dependence of art on physical form and its visual apperception. Conceptualism was a broader attitudinal expression that summarized a wide array of works and practices which, in radically reducing the role of the art object, reimagined the possibilities of art vis-à-vis the social, political, and economic realities within which it was being made.[68]

This is a blatant promotion of conceptualism at the expense of Conceptual Art, one that depends on characterizing it as "essentially formalist"—a reductive falsification, as Mary Kelly's work, for instance, demonstrates beyond any doubt. Nevertheless, *Global Conceptualism* has, over time, encouraged a wave of studies focused on conceptualisms from around the world, each situated relative to pertinent local histories, which in turn reopened Conceptual Art to new kinds of revisionist inquiry attendant to its own geopolitics as well as its identity politics.[69] Now increasingly seen as a landmark exhibition and a turning point in thinking about Conceptual Art and conceptualism, initially *Global Conceptualism* received mixed reviews owing to its massiveness and exhaustive scope. Ken Johnson, writing for the *New York Times*, called *Global Conceptualism* "ambitious and groundbreaking" but also "tedious and confusing" because there was "no continuous narrative movement through the show."[70] Frazer Ward, for *Frieze*, concluded that the exhibition "overreached itself" but "was nonetheless compelling" even if the conceptualism on offer became "too baggy, temporally distended and leaky a category."[71]

Notably, both of these critics lamented the absence of a comprehensive understanding of conceptualism in *Global Conceptualism*. Indeed, this has been slow in coming, despite a scholarly literature on individual conceptualisms that is growing steadily.[72] Though Smith dealt entirely with art from Australia and New Zealand for *Global Conceptualism*, his take on conceptualism, particularly as he expounded it in the exhibition catalog, began a process of advancing, on the basis of his earlier work on Conceptual Art, a general theory of conceptualism of the sort that Johnson and Ward found wanting. "Peripheries in Motion" (also published, in a slightly different and longer version as "Conceptual Art in Transit" in the second volume of Smith's collected essays in *Transformations in Australian Art*) was Smith's contribution to the *Global Conceptualism* catalog.[73] It looks back on the histories of Conceptual Art and conceptualism in Australia and New Zealand (as well as art made by Australians and New Zealanders—himself one of them—living abroad) to propose the salience of travel and, again, translation to that art. Breaking somewhat with the exhibition's stated aim of identifying distinctive "points of origin" for conceptualisms around the world as well as with its proposal of a sharp difference between Conceptual Art and conceptualism, Smith shows how Australians, including Ian Burn, together with New Zealanders such as Billy Apple, shaped the development of Conceptual Art and conceptualism with international practices that drew on their personal movement from place to place, ranging from Sydney and Auckland to New York and London.

Smith's essay centers on accounting historically for "a conceptual questioning of the nature of art" enacted by artists caught up in this matrix.[74] As in his earlier writing on the subject of Conceptual Art, "conceptions of what it is to be an artist" figure prominently, in this case those of a "Romantic, self-expressive" cast, which Smith identifies as prevalent in Australian and New Zealander art from colonization in the late eighteenth century right up to the advent of conceptual and conceptualist approaches in the 1960s.[75] He positions conceptualism within the broader context of colonial and postcolonial history as an art that traveled through empires or former empires and made considerable use of communications media that connected centers and peripheries within them. The exposure to other ways of thinking about art that this afforded, he argues, enabled artists to develop new conceptions of themselves, the activities in which they were partaking, and the results of those activities. Thus, Australians and New Zealanders could shed earlier Romantic commitments in favor of new conceptual ones, and the double consciousness that artists such as Burn and Apple developed as a result of doing so in the spaces between their home countries and their chosen places of expatriation enabled their own distinctive "conceptual work on the concept of art."[76]

In this essay, Smith also proposes a series of chronological stages through which art becomes conceptual that complements the explanatory power of colonialism's spatial logics with a temporal counterpart. These stages, three in number, require first that a culture of radical, experimental, and innovative art—an "avant-garde"—capable of challenging conceptions of art and artist prevail, though it need not be recognizably Conceptual Art.[77] Second, and most crucial for the development of a conceptualism, such a culture had to produce "objects—artworks—that threw perception into doubt" in order to interrogate vision and broach the domain of the conceptual.[78] Finally, subsequent artists had to seize upon this doubt and produce "strategic objects or events" that harnessed the possibility for new modes of perception to change social relations.[79] Smith gives over the majority of his essay to categorizing and examining how these three stages occurred within the local contexts of Australia and New Zealand as well as their consequences for post-conceptual contemporary artists in those countries who subsequently took up the challenges that conceptualism posed.

This three-part account of Conceptual Art's emergence, development, and impact, tied to the importance of questioning conception and perception, carries over into Smith's fullest account of conceptualism to date, the essay "One and Three Ideas," in which the conceptual, political, and geographical concerns of his earlier writings all come together to provide an account of contemporary art's origins. This latest shift in Smith's thinking occurred amid widespread and growing interest in assessing the relationship between conceptualism, still so evidently influential on practicing artists, and contemporary art.[80] Groys's symposium, at which Smith presented the final version of this text, was largely devoted to Moscow Conceptualism, at the time undergoing a resurgence of interest from curators and historians as one of the more prominent conceptualisms to receive scholarly attention in the wake of *Global Conceptualism*. However, the symposium's original title (not retained in its proceedings), "Revisiting Conceptual Art: The Russian Case in an International Context," makes clear that, regardless of the fact that Moscow was isolated in certain respects from other conceptualisms and, therefore, possessed of its own conceptualist "point of origin," scholarship need not restrict discussion of Moscow Conceptualism to the context of the Soviet Union in the 1970s.[81] Indeed, Smith's essay makes significant headway toward a reassessment of the art-historical significance of Moscow Conceptualism by situating conceptualism in general relative to the emergence of contemporaneity as a core value for contemporary art, which he takes to be both global and post-conceptualist in character. The discursive shift proposed here is not only to stop thinking of conceptualism solely in terms of its rejection of a preceding modern (whether modernist, Romantic, or socialist realist) art and its encounters with evolving (capitalist, socialist, or postcolonial) social conditions, but also to insist on conceptualism's salience for the contemporary art that was to come after it. If the entire conceptualist episode, with all its reconceptualization, had one lasting effect, it is, according to Smith, this: to have replaced the modern conception of art, whereby a monolithic historical trajectory locates all art as either fully modern, lagging, or irrelevant, with a contemporary conception of art, according to which there is no one singular trajectory but a plurality of asymmetrical, overlapping, intersecting, or parallel trajectories that each exist contemporaneously with one another and all cohere as a whole by virtue of this contemporaneity.

Support for Smith's idea that conceptualism is intrinsic to the emergence of contemporary art's contemporaneity can be found in Groys's earliest use of the term "conceptualism" to identify something distinct from "Conceptual Art" in his 1979 essay "Moscow Romantic Conceptualism."[82] Against the idea that "'conceptualism' may be understood in the narrower sense as designating a specific artistic movement clearly limited to place, time and origin," Groys defined it "more broadly" as "any attempt to withdraw from the production of artworks as material objects intended for contemplation and aesthetic evaluation and, instead, to thematicize and shape the conditions that determine the viewers' perception of the work of art, the process of its inception by the artist, its positioning in a certain context, and its historical status."[83] This definition has much in common with Smith's own claims from 1974 about Art & Language wanting to break from its Conceptual Art origins in favor of more open conceptions of art, despite the fact that conceptualism in Moscow had limited familiarity with the Conceptual Art in which Smith had participated in New York and elsewhere. Indeed, Groys's formulation contains the same three elements as Smith's definition: a questioning of norms for perceiving art, an effort to make a theme of those norms, and an attempt to actively transform the broader contexts in which they appear as normative.

That independent theories of conceptualism have found themselves staking similar claims is hardly coincidental. Indeed, this confirms the fact that conceptualism, despite its diverse local manifestations, possesses a broader character, and Smith's participation in Groys's symposium provided an opportunity to test precisely this idea.[84] Without dismissing the importance of local configurations of conceptualism, Smith advances an ambitious account of, as his title suggests, conceptualism before, during, and after Conceptual Art that approaches "'a theory of conceptualism.'"[85] The essay draws heavily on his previous three-stage account of art's relation to concepts in the context of Australia and New Zealand by arguing that there "were at least one, usually two, and sometimes three conceptions of conceptualism in play at each moment—and that these were in play, differently although connectedly, in various places, at each of these times."[86] The first—"before" Conceptual Art—corresponds to the "avant-garde" art of the earlier formulation:

> 1. At its various beginnings, conceptualism was a set of practices for interrogating what it was for perceiving subjects and perceived objects to be in the world (that is, it was an inquiry into the minimal situations in which art might be possible).[87]

The second—"during"—parallels his recognition, first made in 1974 and reiterated in 1995 and 1999, of a more radicalized and extreme kind of art such as that of Art & Language or certain work by Kosuth:

> 2. That, as well as being a set of practices for interrogating what it was for perceiving subjects and perceived

> objects to be in the world (that is, it was an inquiry into the minimal situations in which art might be possible), conceptualism was also a further integrated set of practices for interrogating the conditions under which the first interrogation becomes possible and necessary (that is, an inquiry into the maximal conditions for art to be thought).[88]

And the third—"after"—concerns art that investigates the societal contexts in which such practices are ongoing, echoing the political thrust of his earlier third stage:

> 3. The conditions—social, languaged, cultural, and political—of practices (1) and (2) were problematized, as was communicative exchange as such (that is, inquiry became an active engagement in the pragmatic conditions that might generate a defeasible sociality).[89]

These three ways of being conceptualist—one that, historically, precedes and results in Conceptual Art; one that embodies it at its most extreme; and one that suggests a direction forward for art in its wake—generalize the historical circumstances that Smith tracked in "Peripheries in Motion" to propose a broad theory of conceptualism untethered to the specificities of any single local history and centrally preoccupied with conception and reconceiving art and its role in the world. In each of their instantiations, the three propositions can manifest individually, in one of three possible pairs, or all at once—and not necessarily in the order that they did in the Conceptual Art of the 1960s and 1970s. The essay's title, a riff on Kosuth's *One and Three Chairs* and other similarly titled works of his from the 1960s, signifies that conceptualism is simultaneously one thing and three things—or three things that all realize the same process through diverse means and at different intensities: to reconceive what art is and does.

Smith then applies these ideas to the case of Moscow Conceptualism and concludes that (1) and (3) apply to art such as Ilya Kabakov's, which thwarts perceptual expectations and confronts the social conditions of Soviet life at the time, while (2) does not, owing to "a sense that adopting its modes would be irrelevant to local concerns and to local audiences."[90] The Soviet Union did not have an Art & Language

Ilya Kabakov, I Tell Him 'If You Want to Live with Me, Behave Yourself . . .', *1981. Oil on fiberboard, 44½ × 80¼ in. (113 × 203.6 cm). Collection Zimmerli Art Museum at Rutgers Norton and Nancy Dodge Collection of Nonconformist Art from the Soviet Union 1997.0596/08654. © 2015 Artists Rights Society (ARS), New York / VG Bild-Kunst, Bonn. Photo: Jack Abraham.*

group because work like Art & Language's would not contribute to reconceiving what art could be and do in such a society. (Here, Smith's initial foray into thinking about Conceptual Art via a deep investment in Art & Language is rendered totally contingent, a measure of how much his thinking has changed since the 1970s.) The absence of (2) does not disqualify Soviet art from possessing a conceptualism, since (1) and (3) accomplished a shift away from the realist modes pervading the official Soviet art that preceded it toward the globally connected contemporary art produced by Russian and Eastern European artists since. Moscow Conceptualism, analogously to Conceptual Art in the West or comparable art in Japan, China, Africa, and so on, brought art into a new state of global contemporaneity with itself, thereby severing ties to preceding modern contexts for making art.

In the end, Smith concludes that whether or not art like Kabakov's is recognized as conceptual or conceptualist may ultimately be less relevant than whether it is recognized as contemporary:

> Given that Conceptual art was the most radical, avant-garde, innovative, and consequential-seeming art of the time and has retained much of that aura since, [artists outside North America and Western Europe] wanted to expand its definition to include themselves. On the most obvious level of simple fairness, they want to be seen to have been contemporary. This, I suggest, is actually more important to many of those involved than whether or not their art was, or may now be seen to be, conceptual.[91]

Here, conceptualism emerges as a cipher for contemporaneity, and Smith's theory of conceptualism reconceives itself as a history of contemporary art's origins. What might matter most from an art-historical standpoint (as well as for the artists who helped to make recent art history) is that the shift from late modern to contemporary art is recognized as a global one to which artists everywhere contributed and that these contributions themselves constituted the shift from a modern art dominated by European and North American modernisms to a contemporary art that comes to be through the contemporaneity of differences. Conceptualism's ultimate significance, then, in Smith's account, is its role in the shift from modern to contemporary art—this is where it effects its most widespread reconceptualization of art. The result is not a homogeneous and globally shared conception of art but rather a proliferation of different conceptions of art during the latter half of the twentieth century that, because of their conceptualist interest in conception, mutually recognize one another even as they differ. Art came to be contemporary, according to Smith's claim, because artists everywhere began to partake of a worldwide effort to rethink art. Such an effort was, of course, distinctive in each locality, but in its most basic ambition, it was the same: to find new conceptions of art.

A CONCEPTUALIST THEORY OF CONTEMPORARY ART

In its culminating articulation, Smith's theory of conceptualism frames its object as decisive for the historical transition from modern to contemporary art. In so doing, it emerges as a theory of contemporary art's origins. From the list of readily available and widely held accounts of this decisive phenomenon in late twentieth-century art, those such as Smith's that locate conceptualism as both a point of no return for modern art and a point of departure for contemporary art possess certain advantages in that they are able to explain three things that such a theory ought to be able to explain in an interrelated way: first, what conditions modern art, contemporary art's historical predecessor, supplied for its emergence; second, how a worldwide transition from modern to contemporary art occurred; and, finally, what distinguishing features contemporary art possesses that modern art did not (and indeed could not). All of the other leading accounts of this transition struggle to integrate fully one or more of these points. Those positing an "anything-goes" post-historicity as the dominant framework for understanding contemporary art usually disregard the specificities of a distinctly contemporary art by advocating for a blanket pluralism that results from modernist imperatives, which, they theorize at length, had exhausted their historical purpose.[92] Inversely, accounts of contemporary art as the art of a post-1989 global culture tend to overemphasize its engagement with new historical developments while saying less about how it emerged out of modern predecessors with which it has come to differ.[93] Those accounts that insist on theorizing with equal robustness both sides of a divide between the modern and the contemporary usually posit a shift from modernism to postmodernism or from avant-gardes to neo-avant-gardes that is insufficiently global in scope.[94] Smith's theory differs from these for its ability to address the entirety of the transition from modern to contemporary art. Rather than figure conceptualism as a component of this shift, as other theories, where they speak of it, tend to do, Smith theorizes the transition from modern to contemporary art as an act of reconceiving. First, modern art consolidates monolithic and competing conceptions of art such as modernism and socialist realism that generate internal opposition in the form of avant-gardes and other kinds of unofficial culture. This tension drives a number of searches for new conceptions of art, and, finally, the realization of those new conceptions results in a condition of artistic contemporaneity that is incompatible with the universalizing aims of modern art.

This reconceptualization has certain consequences for the relationship between art and historiographical accounting for art. Smith's theory of conceptualism not only accounts for conceptualism theoretically; it also theorizes in a conceptualist manner, and this breaks down the usually clear distinction between art and writing about art. In its final form, the theory is the product of a repeatedly reconceived conception of what conceptualism is that has, over time, partaken of the major twists and turns in the histories and historiographies of both Conceptual Art and conceptualism. Ultimately, it reconceives itself as a theory of contemporary art's origins and reconceives those very origins by refusing to align with other conceptions of them. That process began in 1974 when "Art and Art and Language" challenged the emerging consensus about Conceptual Art by asserting that the concept of conception could sustain further conceptual investigations into the concept of art. "The Tasks of Translation" returned to Conceptual Art during a moment of retrospective attention to propose further that Conceptual Art was not merely interested in conception but in reconceiving conceptions. "A Conversation on Conceptual Art, Subjectivity and the *Post-Partum Document*" uncovered the political stakes in such an endeavor amid a wider effort to revise understanding of Conceptual Art where its politics are concerned. Similarly, "Peripheries in Motion" identifies Conceptual Art's geographical stakes within a newly recognized and vast conceptualism in the art of the world after midcentury. And, finally, "One and Three Ideas" pulls all of this together to stake a powerful claim about the salience of conceptualism for contemporary art at a time when its ongoing relevance continues to be up for grabs. That the theory has persisted through each of these major changes in how Conceptual Art and conceptualism have been circumscribed demonstrates the ongoing relevance of its central claims for continuing efforts to understand (and thereby extend) important episodes in the recent history of art, especially an artistic tendency that has, from its beginnings, and in concert with a historiography that shares its predilections, been devoted to rethinking how art can be thought—and how thought can be art.

NOTES

1. The standard history of Art & Language remains Charles Harrison's *Essays on Art & Language* (Cambridge, MA: MIT Press, 2001) and its companion volume, Charles Harrison, *Conceptual Art and Painting: Further Essays on Art & Language* (Cambridge, MA: MIT Press, 2003).

2. On the New York section of the collective, see Michael Corris, "Inside a New York Art Gang: Selected Documents of Art & Language, New York" (1996), in Alexander Alberro and Blake Stimson, eds., *Conceptual Art: A Critical Anthology* (Cambridge, MA: MIT Press, 1999), 471–85; Christopher Gilbert, "Art & Language, New York, Discusses Its Social Relations in 'The Lumpen-Headache,'" in Michael Corris, ed., *Conceptual Art: Theory, Practice, and Myth* (Cambridge: Cambridge University Press, 2004), 326–41; and Chris Gilbert, "Art & Language and the Institutional Form in Anglo-American Collectivism," in Blake Stimson and Gregory Sholette, eds., *Collectivism after Modernism:*

The Art of Social Imagination after 1945 (Minneapolis: University of Minnesota Press, 2007), 77–93.

3. For Art & Language projects in which Smith played a substantial role, see Art & Language, *Blurting in A&L* (New York and Halifax: Art & Language Press and the Press of the Nova Scotia College of Art, 1973); Ian Burn, Mel Ramsden, and Terry Smith, "Draft for an Anti-Textbook," *Art-Language* 3, no. 1 (September 1974); and Terry Smith, ed., *Art & Language Australia* (Banbury, UK: Art & Language Press, 1976).

4. Terry Smith, "Color-Form Painting: Sydney 1967–1970," *Other Voices* 1, no. 1 (June–July 1970): 6–17.

5. For the catalog accompanying this exhibition, see Terry Smith and Tony McGillick, *The Situation Now: Object or Post-Object Art?* (Sydney: Contemporary Art Society of Australia, 1971).

6. Terry Smith, "Art and Art and Language," *Artforum* (February 1974): 49–52.

7. Smith, "Art and Art and Language," 49.

8. Smith, "Art and Art and Language," 49.

9. For the edition of Kuhn that Art & Language read, see Thomas S. Kuhn, *The Structure of Scientific Revolutions*, 2nd ed. (Chicago: University of Chicago Press, 1970).

10. For Smith's earlier writings on provincialism, see especially Terry Smith, "The Provincialism Problem," *Artforum* (September 1974): 54–59, but also the earlier Terry Smith, "Provincialism in Art," *Quadrant* (April 1971): 67–71. Also worth reading is an essay, predating both of these texts, by Smith's colleague in Art & Language, Ian Burn, "Art Is What We Do, Culture Is What We Do to Other Artists," in *Dialogue: Writings in Art History* (Sydney: Allen and Unwin, 1991), 131–39. On the historiography of provincialism, see Heather Barker and Charles Green, "The Provincialism Problem: Terry Smith and Center-Periphery Art History," *Journal of Art Historiography* 3 (December 2010): 1–17.

11. A number of transcripts from the discussions in Melbourne and Adelaide are collected in Smith, *Art & Language Australia.*

12. Terry Smith, "The Tasks of Translation: Art & Language in Australia & New Zealand 1975–6," in Ian Wedde and Gregory Burke, eds., *Now See Hear! Art, Language and Translation* (Wellington, New Zealand: Victoria University Press, 1990), 253–54.

13. Mary Kelly and Terry Smith, "A Conversation about Conceptual Art, Subjectivity and the *Post-Partum Document*" (1995), in Alberro and Stimson, *Conceptual Art*, 450–58.

14. Kelly and Smith, "Conversation about Conceptual Art," 451.

15. Luis Camnitzer, Jane Farver, and Rachel Weiss, eds., "Foreword," in *Global Conceptualism: Points of Origin, 1950s–1980s* (New York: Queens Museum of Art, 1999), viii.

16. Terry Smith, "Peripheries in Motion: Conceptualism and Conceptual Art in Australia and New Zealand," in Camnitzer, Farver, and Weiss, *Global Conceptualism*, 87.

17. For Smith's work on contemporary art and contemporaneity to date, see especially Terry Smith, *What Is Contemporary Art?* (Chicago: University of Chicago Press, 2009); Terry Smith, *Contemporary Art: World Currents* (Upper Saddle River, NJ: Pearson / Prentice Hall, 2011); and Terry Smith, *Thinking Contemporary Curating* (New York: Independent Curators International, 2012).

18. Terry Smith, "One and Three Ideas: Conceptualism Before, During, and After Conceptual Art," in Boris Groys, ed., *Moscow Symposium: Conceptualism Revisited* (Berlin: Sternberg, 2012), 42–72.

19. Smith, "One and Three Ideas," 46.

20. For ties between Conceptual Art and the radical politics of the 1960s, see Blake Stimson, "The Promise of Conceptual Art," in Alberro and Stimson, *Conceptual Art*, xxxviii–lii; and Julia Bryan-Wilson, *Art Workers: Radical Practice in the Vietnam War Era* (Berkeley: University of California Press, 2011). For Conceptual Art's relationship to other intellectual currents in the 1960s and 1970s, see, on poststructuralism and psychoanalysis, Eve Meltzer, *Systems We Have Loved: Conceptual Art, Affect, and the Antihumanist Turn* (Chicago: University of Chicago Press, 2013); on information theory, cybernetics, and computing, Edward A. Shanken, "Art in the Information Age: Technology and Conceptual Art," *Leonardo* 35, no. 4 (August 2002): 433–38; and, on systems theory, Luke Skrebowski, "All Systems Go: Recovering Hans Haacke's Systems Aesthetics," *Grey Room* 30 (August 2008): 54–83.

21. Lucy R. Lippard and John Chandler, "The Dematerialization of Art" (1968), in Alberro and Stimson, *Conceptual Art*, 46. Lippard's book *Six Years: The Dematerialization of the Art Object . . .* (New York: Praeger, 1973) is among the first book-length treatments of Conceptual Art, and it develops ideas first posed in the essay she wrote with Chandler while also looking back retrospectively at the fate of dematerialization.

22. Lippard and Chandler, "Dematerialization of Art," 46.

23. Sol LeWitt, "Paragraphs on Conceptual Art" (1967), in Alberro and Stimson, *Conceptual Art*, 12. (Alberro and Stimson mistakenly give "of" where LeWitt originally wrote "or.")

24. Sol LeWitt, "Sentences on Conceptual Art" (1969), in Alberro and Stimson, *Conceptual Art*, 107.

25. Joseph Kosuth, "Art after Philosophy" (1969), in Alberro and Stimson, *Conceptual Art*, 171.

26. The tautological quality of Kosuth's early writings about Conceptual Art has been much criticized. See, in particular, Benjamin H. D. Buchloh, "Conceptual Art 1962–1969: From the Aesthetic of Administration to the Critique of Institutions," *October* 55 (Winter 1990): 105–43. See also Joseph Kosuth and Seth Siegelaub, "Joseph Kosuth and Seth Siegelaub Reply to Ben-

jamin Buchloh on Conceptual Art," *October* 57 (Summer 1991): 152–57, as well as Benjamin Buchloh, "Buchloh Replies to Kosuth and Seth Siegelaub," *October* 57 (Summer 1991): 158–61.

27. Kosuth, "Art after Philosophy," 164.

28. Kosuth, "Art after Philosophy," 171. Emphasis in original.

29. Both Peter Osborne and Alexander Alberro follow Kosuth in drawing internal distinctions of kind within Conceptual Art. See Osborne's differentiation between "*inclusive* or *weak* Conceptualists" and "*exclusive* or *strong* Conceptualists" in Peter Osborne, "Conceptual Art and/as Philosophy," in Michael Newman and Jon Bird, eds., *Rewriting Conceptual Art* (London: Reaktion, 1999), 49. For Osborne on Conceptual Art more generally, see Peter Osborne, *Conceptual Art* (London: Phaidon, 2002). See also Alexander Alberro, "Reconsidering Conceptual Art, 1966–1977," in Alberro and Stimson, *Conceptual Art*, xvi–xxxvii, for a more finely grained set of distinctions.

30. On these exhibitions, see Alison M. Green, "*When Attitudes Become Form* and the Contest over Conceptual Art's History," in Corris, *Conceptual Art*, 123–43; Ken Allan, "Understanding *Information*," in Corris, *Conceptual Art*, 144–68; Florence Dereux, *Harald Szeemann: Individual Methodology* (Zürich: JRP | Ringier, 2007), 91–148; and Christian Rattemeyer and other authors, *Exhibiting the New Art: "Op Losse Schroeven" and "When Attitudes Become Form" 1969* (London: Afterall, 2010). For these anthologies, see Ursula Meyer, ed., *Conceptual Art* (New York: Dutton, 1972); Lippard, *Six Years*; and Gregory Battcock, ed., *Idea Art: A Critical Anthology* (New York: Dutton, 1973).

31. Smith, "Art and Art and Language," 52.

32. Smith, "Art and Art and Language," 49.

33. Smith, "Art and Art and Language," 49.

34. In this regard, see especially Art & Language, *Comparative Models* (1972), in Art & Language, *Art & Language* (Eindhoven, Netherlands: Van Abbemuseum, 1980), 51–62.

35. Smith, "Art and Art and Language," 49. Four years earlier, Terry Atkinson, also a participant in Art & Language, had similarly sought to distinguish Art & Language's "point of view" from that of other conceptual artists. See Terry Atkinson, "From an Art & Language Point of View," *Art-Language* 1, no. 2 (February 1970): 25–60.

36. Kosuth, "Art after Philosophy," 172.

37. Smith, "Art and Art and Language," 50.

38. Smith, "Art and Art and Language," 50.

39. See Claude Gintz, *L'art conceptuel, une perspective* (Paris: Musée d'Art Moderne de la Ville de Paris, 1989).

40. For Buchloh's formula, see Buchloh, "Conceptual Art 1962–1969," 107, which previously appeared, in an earlier version, in Gintz, *L'art conceptuel*. For Harrison's approach, see Charles Harrison, "Art Object and Art Work," in

Gintz, *L'art conceptuel*, 64. Harrison elaborates further on this idea in the second chapter of Harrison, *Essays on Art & Language*.

41. Buchloh, "Conceptual Art 1962–1969," 143. For further elaborations upon the historical contexts in which conceptual artists worked, see Alexander Alberro, *Conceptual Art and the Politics of Publicity* (Cambridge: MIT Press, 2003), which considers the key role of the dealer Seth Siegelaub; and Sophie Richard, *Unconcealed: The International Network of Conceptual Artists 1967–77: Dealers, Exhibitions and Public Collections* (London: Ridinghouse, 2009), which reconstructs much of the original patronage for conceptual artists.

42. On institutional critique, see in particular John C. Welchmann, ed., *Institutional Critique and After* (Zürich: JRP | Ringier, 2006); Alexander Alberro and Blake Stimson, eds., *Institutional Critique: An Anthology of Artists' Writings* (Cambridge, MA: MIT Press, 2009); and Gerald Raunig and Gene Ray, eds., *Art and Contemporary Critical Practice: Reinventing Institutional Critique* (London: MayFly, 2009). Incidentally, Mel Ramsden seems to have coined the term "institutional critique," albeit as a term of derision, writing in *The Fox* in 1975, "to dwell perennially on an institutional critique without addressing specific problems within the institutions is to generalize and sloganize." See Mel Ramsden, "On Practice," in Alberro and Stimson, *Institutional Critique*, 176. See Alexander Alberro's discussion of this in Alexander Alberro, "Institutions, Critique, and Institutional Critique," in Alberro and Stimson, *Institutional Critique*, 8.

43. Smith, "Tasks of Translation," 254.

44. Ian Burn, "Looking through a Piece of Glass: Some Early Conceptualist Concerns," in Wedde and Burke, *Now See Hear!*, 209.

45. Burn, "Looking through a Piece of Glass," 209.

46. For the textual portion of *Soft-Tape*, see Art & Language, *Art & Language*, 17–18.

47. Smith's essay is reproduced in this volume. On *Soft-Tape*, see also Michiel Dolk, "It's Only Art Conceptually: A Consideration of the Work of Ian Burn, 1965–1970," in *Ian Burn: Minimal-Conceptual Work* (Perth: Art Gallery of Western Australia, 1992), 17–44; and Ann Stephen, "Soft Talk/*Soft-Tape*: The Early Collaborations of Ian Burn and Mel Ramsden," in Corris, *Conceptual Art*, 80–97. Stephen is highly critical of Smith's claims about the relationship between *Soft-Tape* and his work in Art & Language, though her criticisms are not always well sourced or cited. See especially Stephen, "Soft Talk/*Soft-Tape*," 81 and 94n5.

48. Burn, "Looking through a Piece of Glass," 209.

49. Burn, "Looking through a Piece of Glass," 209.

50. Burn, "Looking through a Piece of Glass," 209.

51. Smith, "Art and Art and Language," 50.

52. Smith, "Art and Art and Language," 51.

53. Smith, "Art and Art and Language," 51–52.

54. Members of Art & Language were, during the early 1970s, avid readers of Paul Feyerabend's ideas about incommensurability and epistemological anarchy. See especially Paul Feyerabend, *Against Method* (London: Verso, 1975), which collects a number of earlier writings that Art & Language discussed as a group during the early 1970s. While in California during the spring of 1974, Smith took Feyerabend's graduate course on the pre-Socratic thinkers at the University of California, Berkeley, and he visited the Thomas S. Kuhn Archives housed there.

55. For an insightful account of how art might be possible in the absence of a well-formulated conception, see Richard Shiff, "Same Change," in Karen Painter and Thomas Crow, eds., *Late Thoughts: Reflections on Artists and Composers at Work* (Los Angeles: Getty Research Institute, 2006), 37–53, which examines the case of the elderly Willem de Kooning, who may have suffered from Alzheimer's disease. See especially the section of Shiff's essay entitled "Studio without Concepts," in which he writes, "The hand remains; one loses the concept. But in de Kooning's view, concepts were absurd; he needed none (so he believed) and did everything to remove their influence. By his own conception of art, loss of his full capacity to conceptualize would have had little bearing on his practice" (40).

56. For a sampling of the diverse retrospective views taken by its current and former participants regarding this period in Art & Language's history, see, in addition to Charles Harrison's many writings, Art & Language, "We Aimed to Be Amateurs," *Art-Language* (new series) 2 (June 1997): 40–49; Terry Atkinson, *Indexing, the World War I Moves and the Ruins of Conceptualism* (Manchester, UK: Cornhouse, 1992); and Ian Burn, "The 'Sixties: Crisis and Aftermath (or the Memoirs of an Ex-Conceptual Artist)" (1981), in Alberro and Stimson, *Conceptual Art*, 392–408.

57. See, in particular, the final section of essays collected in Alberro and Stimson, *Conceptual Art*, 504–62, under the heading "Critical Histories of Conceptual Art," as well as anthologies of essays on Conceptual Art, including Bird and Newman, *Rewriting Conceptual Art*, and Corris, *Conceptual Art*.

58. Diarmuid Costello and Margaret Iversen, eds., *Photography after Conceptual Art* (Oxford: Wiley-Blackwell, 2010), provides a number of perspectives on photography. John Roberts, ed., *The Impossible Document: Photography and Conceptual Art in Britain 1966–1976* (London: Camerawork, 1997), and Matthew S. Witkovsky, ed., *Light Years: Conceptual Art and the Photograph, 1964–1977* (Chicago: Art Institute of Chicago, 2012), include additional perspectives.

59. On romantic conceptualism, see Ellen Seifermann and Jörg Heiser, *Romantischer Konzeptualismus/Romantic Conceptualism* (Bielefeld, Germany: Kerber Verlag, 2007), and Peter Eleey, *The Quick and the Dead* (Minneapolis, MN: Walker Art Center, 2009). Boris Groys effectively coined the term in Boris Groys, "Moscow Romantic Conceptualism," in *History Becomes Form:*

Moscow Conceptualism (Cambridge, MA: MIT Press, 2010), 35–56. For a more philosophical understanding of romanticism, see Peter Osborne, "An Image of Romanticism: Fragment and Project in Friedrich Schlegel's *Athenaeum Fragments* and Sol LeWitt's *Sentences on Conceptual Art*," in *Sol LeWitt's Sentences on Conceptual Art: Manuscript and Draft Materials 1968–69* (Oslo: Office for Contemporary Art Norway, 2009), 5–27.

60. Buchloh, "Conceptual Art 1962–1969," 107.

61. Harrison, "Art Object and Artwork," 63.

62. Another part of the discussion, which covers Kelly's 1992 work *Gloria Patri*, appears in Mary Kelly and Terry Smith, "*Gloria Patri*: A Conversation about Power, Sexuality and War," in Terry Smith, ed., *In Visible Touch: Modernism and Masculinity* (Sydney and Chicago: Power Institute and University of Chicago Press, 1997), 233–51.

63. On *Post-Partum Document*, see Mary Kelly, *Post-Partum Document* (Berkeley: University of California Press, 1999).

64. Kelly and Smith, "Conversation about Conceptual Art," 450, 451.

65. Kelly and Smith, "Conversation about Conceptual Art," 451.

66. On Art & Language's political collaborations, see Corris, "Inside a New York Art Gang."

67. Kelly and Smith, "Conversation about Conceptual Art," 452.

68. Camnitzer, Farver, and Weiss, "Foreword," viii.

69. On Conceptual Art's geographies, see Christophe Cherix, *In and Out of Amsterdam: Travels in Conceptual Art, 1960–1976* (New York: Museum of Modern Art, 2009), which examines the vital role Amsterdam played in Conceptual Art circles, largely for artists from outside the city; and Richard, *Unconcealed*, which shows how a cosmopolitan web of participants wove together a fabric that helped institutionalize Conceptual Art by connecting it to the art market. On Conceptual Art and identity politics, particularly concerning gender and race, see Jayne Wark, "Conceptual Art and Feminism: Martha Rosler, Adrian Piper, Eleanor Antin, and Martha Wilson," *Women's Art Journal* 22, no. 1 (Spring–Summer 2001), 44–50; Valerie Cassel Oliver, ed., *Double Consciousness: Black Conceptual Art since 1970* (Houston, TX: Contemporary Arts Museum, 2006); Kobena Mercer, "Adrian Piper, 1970–1975: Exiled on Main Street," and Amna Malik, "Conceptualising 'Black' British Art through the Lens of Exile," in Kobena Mercer, ed., *Exiles, Diasporas, and Strangers* (Cambridge, MA, and London: MIT Press and InIVA, 2008), 146–65, 166–89; John P. Bowles, *Adrian Piper: Race, Gender, and Embodiment* (Durham, NC: Duke University Press, 2011); and Cornelia Butler and other authors, *From Conceptualism to Feminism: Lucy Lippard's Numbers Shows 1969–74* (London: Afterall, 2012).

70. Ken Johnson, "Conceptual but Verbal, Very Verbal," *New York Times*, May 7, 1999, 36.

71. Frazer Ward, "Global Conceptualism: Points of Origin, 1950s–1980s,"

Frieze 48 (September–October 1999), http://www.frieze.com/issue/review/global_conceptualism_points_of_origin_1950s_1980s/.

72. A few highlights from the literatures on conceptualisms include Luis Camnitzer, *Conceptualism in Latin American Art: Didactics of Liberation* (Austin: University of Texas Press, 2007); Salah M. Hassan and Olu Oguibe, eds., *Authentic/Ex-Centric: Conceptualism in Contemporary African Art* (Ithaca, NY: Forum for African Arts, 2001); Miško Šuvaković, "Conceptual Art," in Dubravka Djurić and Miško Šuvaković, eds., *Impossible Histories: Historical Avant-Gardes, Neo-Avant-Gardes, and Post-Avant-Gardes in Yugoslavia, 1918–1991* (Cambridge, MA: MIT Press, 2003), 210–45; and Groys, *History Becomes Form*.

73. For the longer version of the essay, see Terry Smith, "Conceptual Art in Transit," in *Transformations in Australian Art*, vol. 2: *The Twentieth Century—Modernism and Aboriginality* (Sydney: Craftsman House, 2002), 122–43.

74. Smith, "Peripheries in Motion," 87.

75. Smith, "Peripheries in Motion," 87.

76. Smith, "Peripheries in Motion," 88.

77. Smith, "Peripheries in Motion," 88. For Smith on the need for an avant-garde in Australia, see Terry Smith, "Propositions" (1971), in Alberro and Stimson, *Conceptual Art*, 258–61.

78. Smith, "Peripheries in Motion," 88.

79. Smith, "Peripheries in Motion," 89.

80. Peter Osborne's *Anywhere or Not at All: Philosophy of Contemporary Art* (London: Verso, 2013) includes a claim to the effect that "contemporary art *is* post-conceptual art" (19). For the origins of this claim in the idea that Conceptual Art is a "vanishing mediator" between the art that precedes and antecedes it, see Osborne, "Conceptual Art and/as Philosophy," 64–65. See also Alexander Alberro and Sabeth Buchmann, eds., *Art after Conceptual Art* (Cambridge, MA, and Vienna: MIT Press and Generali Foundation, 2006), and Camiel Van Winkel, *During the Exhibition the Gallery Will Be Closed: Contemporary Art and the Paradoxes of Conceptualism* (Amsterdam: Valiz, 2012).

81. On Moscow Conceptualism, see, in addition to the proceedings of Groys's symposium and Groys, *History Becomes Form*, Matthew Jesse Jackson, *The Experimental Group: Ilya Kabakov, Moscow Conceptualism, Soviet Avant-Garde* (Chicago: University of Chicago Press, 2010), and Alla Rosenfeld, ed., *Moscow Conceptualism in Context* (New York: Prestel, 2011).

82. Of his use of the term "conceptualism," Groys has written, "It was said time and again that I had not used this term in its precise sense because the term 'conceptual art' designates primarily the practice of the group 'Art & Language' and of Joseph Kosuth—and Moscow conceptualist art production does not look like that of Kosuth. However, I myself said precisely that at the beginning of 'Moscow Romantic Conceptualism.'" See Groys, *History Becomes Form*, 7.

83. Groys, "Moscow Romantic Conceptualism," 35.

84. Smith presented earlier versions of this paper in Toronto in November 2010 and in London in March 2011. It first appeared in print in *e-flux journal* 29 (November 2011), http://www.e-flux.com/journal/one-and-three-ideas-conceptualism-before-during-and-after-conceptual-art/.

85. Smith, "One and Three Ideas," 51.

86. Smith, "One and Three Ideas," 46.

87. Smith, "One and Three Ideas," 51.

88. Smith, "One and Three Ideas," 57.

89. Smith, "One and Three Ideas," 58.

90. Smith, "One and Three Ideas," 63.

91. Smith, "One and Three Ideas," 66–67.

92. On the end of art, see Arthur Danto, *After the End of Art: Contemporary Art and the Pale of History* (Princeton, NJ: Princeton University Press, 1998).

93. On contemporary art as a global art, see the range of perspectives in Hans Belting and Andrea Buddensieg, eds., *The Global Contemporary and the Rise of New Art Worlds* (Cambridge, MA: MIT Press, 2013).

94. For an account of a shift from modernism to postmodernism mediated by the emergence of a post-medium condition, see Rosalind Krauss, *A Voyage on the North Sea: Art in the Age of the Post-Medium Condition* (London: Thames and Hudson, 2000). On the neo-avant-garde, see Benjamin H. D. Buchloh, *Neo-Avantgarde and Culture Industry* (Cambridge, MA: MIT Press, 2000); Benjamin H. D. Buchloh, *Formalism and Historicity: Models and Methods in Twentieth-Century Art* (Cambridge, MA: MIT Press, 2015); and Hal Foster, *The Return of the Real* (Cambridge, MA: MIT Press, 1996).

1 Art and Art and Language

For more than a year various writers in this magazine, and others, have referred to the Art & Language group of artists. Their remarks add up to a sorry list of misunderstandings, distortions, and hasty judgments, interspersed with occasional expressions of tentative and somewhat puzzled sympathy, that typify the reception of Art & Language work in this country. Part of the reason follows from the nature of Art & Language work itself: its modes of address and most of what it has to say are not only new and unfamiliar, but new and unfamiliar in ways which are themselves foreign to the art audience here.

Thus, it becomes important to give an accounting of the Art & Language point of view—or, more accurately, of my understanding of it. I should say immediately that I acquired my conception during the past year, as I moved from observing Art & Language (A&L) as an art critic to active participation in the A&L inquiry.

Approaching A&L from within the framework of beliefs and expectations current in the art world, one might feel that here are a group of artists making destructive, extraordinary, often contradictory, and, perhaps, deceitful claims for their work. How can their typewritten essays be considered visual art? Why is their writing style so obscure? Are they trying to do philosophy of language or are they parodying philosophers? How does their work fit in with other Conceptual Art? Are they simply artists taking on the roles of art critics and art theorists? Do they really believe that they can "clean up" the theoretical confusions rife in art discourse so that we all might be able to make "theoretically more sound" art at some future time?

These questions can be easily countered in the rhetorical, polemical style typical of art-world debate. And some of A&L's replies to criticism have been of this order. But it interests me more to propose a description of the A&L point of view *alternative* to those these questions presuppose. To begin doing so, I need to outline reasons why A&L seems so pertinent.

My openness to A&L started from the broad view I took of the current state of art. It seemed to me that the condition of art was—as it remains—disastrous. And not because of the announcement of the "death of painting" on every corner; or because a systematic style had failed to succeed Minimalism; nor finally because of some kind of "failure of sensibility" that had mysteriously afflicted all the practicing artists of the world. Rather, insofar as these and other fears had any sense at all, they were symptoms of a deeper shift from certain fundamental conceptions of what it is to make art, to be an artist, and to understand art. It seemed imperative to determine what these conceptions were, how they related to one another, how they functioned in other contexts, and how they so thoroughly informed the making of art. Furthermore it seemed obvious that trying to create yet more art objects ("thinking in paint"), or conjuring up still more ingenious art-critical theories, was to do no more than to desperately strive to "save the theory." Yet much Conceptual or "Art-as-Idea" art of the past few years willfully compounds this problem-set by using *it* as material for art. Most recent criticism has shown itself inadequate precisely because it refuses to surrender the self-imposed limitation that it dance attendance on what the artists do. (A critic can always wait, saying: "There are hundreds of thousands of artists out there, all dedicated to producing the best art they can—how can I say that some of them, at some future time, won't come up with the goods?" Artists can only partially take this option; finally, an artist has to act *through* an art-making situation, or give up entirely.)

As the necessary tools were not to be found in current art and art-critical practices, it seemed natural to turn to that aspect of philosophy which addressed itself to the expression of concepts in language. It was equally natural to turn to the philosophy of science because this is a field of inquiry consumed in controversy—what it is to do science and what it is to do the philosophy of science. These controversies might, perhaps, throw some light on those debilitating the art world. It became clear to me that the making of art entailed the holding of a set of theories about art (to which T. S. Kuhn's notion of paradigm seems only an approximate analogy), theory-sets constituted by notions of what the world is like.[1]

A formalist artist and critic, insofar as his beliefs are consistent, holds intuitionist ideas of the immanent properties of things, "empirical" attitudes to the experientiality of his products, and a theory of autonomy guiding the self-definitional nature of his artworks as well as their place in an immanently developing history and future of art in general. Other artists have assumptions which cluster around a romantic subjectivism, adding another version of autonomy which aims to secure the uniqueness of themselves and their products, along with a "special" status for their insights within the society at large. Still other artists emphasize theories that artworks are essentially physical objects with a necessarily material character, and believe that sacred among the rituals of producing artworks is the activity of making ("manipulating stuff," "displaying processes"). Obviously, these notions are held with varying degrees of self-consciousness, are rarely systematized beyond random "right intuitions," and appear in many interwoven and differently emphasized guises. But, nonetheless, in my view they amount to the overall theoretical framework within which all art activity is conducted; they individually constitute "deep" concepts of art for those who hold them, generating the different points of view which we see operating during controversies; and, most importantly, they are *in* the artworks, governing their form and content.

It hardly matters to any artist that the theories constituting these theory-sets are being shown in philosophy to be seriously flawed. "Good art from bad theory" is a slogan which can be decked out with many illustrious names. My point is that the negative side of this half-truth has recently come into play: as the structural power of these theory-sets becomes more overt, their inherent inadequacies become unavoidable, with the result that they foreclose on activity derived from them.

The key cause of art's misfortune is that, through the past decade, each one of these theory-sets, having initially clustered together to form open concepts of art for those who employed them, have become progressively more closed, fixed, and over-determined through continual usage and ever more refined self-definition. They no longer have the generative power of "essentially contested concepts": all-too-clear criteria for their "proper" use have been developed.[2]

The paucity of invention and the puerility of talk in the current art world is a direct result of this situation. Basic beliefs, fundamental features of one's concept of art, stand revealed as anomalies within a whole too easily grasped, or ungraspable. Superficial changes, in "style" for example, become trivial when the foundations are shaking.

A glance through some of the better-known A&L essays will reveal that a critique of this sort (although not as wide-ranging and total) was being developed during the later 1960s, and continues.[3] The A&L critique includes a notion perhaps more disturbing than any which I have offered so far: that the anomalous features of the various concepts of art are incorrigible in principle. The suggestion here is that none of the concepts capture anything *natural* to the practice of art because nothing is natural to that practice—rather, they are merely *conventions* adopted by artists as if they were natural. None of them are essential, they are all expendable, all relative to time and place. It is this, rather than any distaste for "objects" per se, which limits any application to the visual arts of Victor Burgin's suggestion to architects:

> Perhaps it is time for a moratorium on *things*—a temporary withdrawal from real objects during which the object analogue formed in consciousness may be examined as the origin of a new generating system.[4]

The situation won't be righted by stepping back in order to get one's "theoretical support structure" into good shape, and then returning to the fray ready to make fundamentally the same kind of art, albeit in some sense "improved." Nor will it be righted by dropping the anomalies, or even by heightening them as the rule of practice. It may well be that, in the long run, it will not be righted at all. Or, if you want to employ analogies from Kuhn's paradigms in science, while it might be possible to show that art has recently shifted *from* one paradigm (or set of paradigms), it cannot be shown that a new paradigm has developed for artists to shift *to*.[5]

In these circumstances, A&L hardly appears from the wings on a white charger waving the banner of its own activity as an alternative form of art—nor, indeed, as an alternative *to* art. What, then, does A&L see itself to be doing? A simple formula answer to this question is not available; nor should we expect it to be. Like any human activity, A&L's is complex and many-sided; it has also been subject to change—constantly on surface levels, occasionally in radical depth. As I see it, the first radical change arose out of the instincts and practices of mid-'60s Conceptual Art to become a distinctively A&L set of intentions: *to construct*

VOLUME I NUMBER I MAY 1969

Art-Language

The Journal of conceptual art

Edited by Terry Atkinson, David Bainbridge, Michael Baldwin, Harold Hurrell

Contents

Art-Language *is published three times a year by Art & Language Press 84 Jubilee Crescent, Coventry CV6 3ET England, to which address all mss and letters should be sent. Price 7s.6d UK, $1.50 USA*

Printed in Great Britain

Art & Language, Art-Language *1, no. 1 (May 1969), cover.*

a complex methodology for nonspecialist critical discourse which would function in the "interstices" between some of the concepts and procedures raised thus far within specialisms such as art, philosophy, sociology, etc. The approaches used were, for example, relativism, "theory-trying," recursivity, and falsification. This first shift began in late 1968, early 1969, and is symbolized by the founding of the journal *Art-Language.* The current point of view differs as a result of responding to the difficulties, accumulating during the last three years, involved in realizing such a program. The concern now is focused more on *exploring the logical, linguistic, and psychological sets which appear to be problematic in considering the possibility of a program such as the initial one*—including, of course, consideration of its potential impossibility. It is, as a 1971 memo puts it, "a body of discourse that literally just searches; out of that 'search' for what is necessary there is a form of skepticism in modality arrived at (or not) in this way."

Perhaps the above concedes too much to the impulse of any "team performer" to display a united external front. Like any other group activity, dissent rather than consensus is internally typical—all notions, including (perhaps especially) those about the A&L point of view, are essentially contested concepts within A&L discussions.[6] The proper use of concepts involves endless dispute about their proper use. This should start to indicate that the inquiry as a whole is not systematic, that it does not study objects in the world external to it and capable of providing "objective" adequacy criteria. It accepts no empirical tests for its sentences, no analytic axioms. Its criteria and modalities are discovered in process, generated by the "search," and are all, in principle, regarded as ad hoc. A&L's frequent use of material from established disciplines is heuristic—no obligations are necessarily felt to the material's previous context of use.

A key characteristic of A&L work is its conversational thrust. The current focal concern is with the implications of various proposals for mapping the semantics and the ideologies of the intersubjective exchange which constitute these conversations. Charles Harrison's essay "Mapping and Filing," and Atkinson/Baldwin's "The Index" give clear accounts of some such proposals (*The New Art*, Hayward Gallery, London, August–September 1972). Of more intensive concern is the idiolectic dictionary currently being compiled by various English members of A&L, and the "Annotations," an exchange of written and verbal commentary, currently being pursued by A&L members in New York.[7]

I cannot summarize this work, but I can give a partial impression of

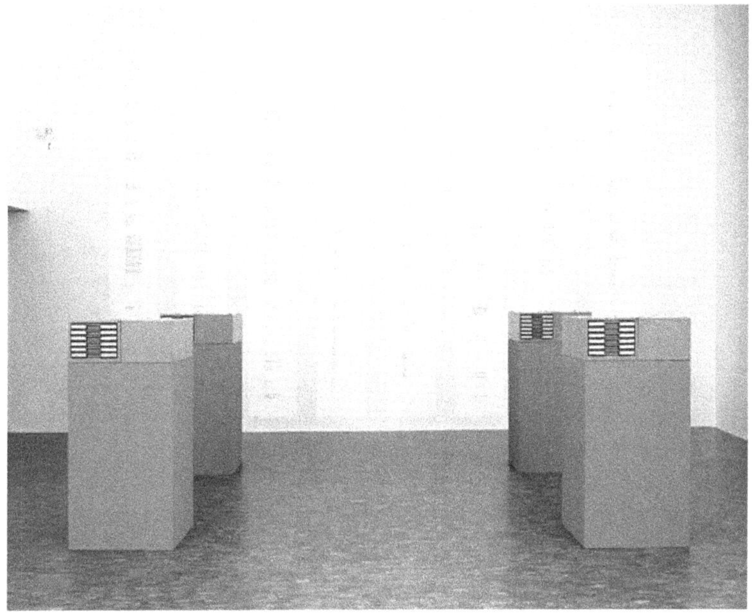

Art & Language, Index 01, *1972. Installation. Eight file cabinets, 48 photostats, texts pasted to walls. Private collection.*

the character of some of the conversations by citing excerpts from notes sent to me in relation to writing this essay:

> [Early] A&L seemed concerned to discuss, in conversation, the problem of the fundamentality of language (or language-dependent items), in relation to prepositional attitudes instantiated in contexts of criticism. . . . [There was a] programmatic concern with the reductions suggested particularly in "ordinary language" linguistic philosophy and in the philosophy of science. . . . [This did not mean] theory-trying, [nor did it] entail a reference-class, e.g. "field of study." . . . One wasn't trying to provide an epistemology as aesthetics, or vice-versa. . . . There was the strain of not seeing the discourse at the opposite end of the cultural continuum from, e.g., the discourse of the scientific community.
>
> Our position at one stage may have been that of a cate-

gory analysis of languages. A metaphysical revision of the language at a Sellars sort of level. This, one suspects, was the surface of something more basic, from an ideological point of view. The requirements of a theory of art seemed in some basic way related to those of a theory of language (or a theory of the possibility of language). We believed that, except in some ideologically remote ways, a theory of this kind was a purely descriptive device. A hermeneutic aspect to the work, engaged with the idea of theoria, and thus to some extent prescriptive/prospective. . . .

The present state of the art might be said to be concerned with dealing with the problem of our context, the kinds of entailments that might exist in our social system, the network of our interpersonal relations—manifest in interactions, certain representative types of interactions regarded as central to the understanding of ideological, political and moral matters. . . . [However] one can't assume that the discourse functions in only one way, even though one might want to point to some primary functions, or note that specializations occur. . . . One breaks with traditional philosophy's assumption that discourse functions in a restricted number of ways and always serves the same purpose, i.e., to do something like convey thoughts.

One is not dealing with out-and-out epistemology. Rather, the development of a semantics adequate to dealing with problems—that one's situation is problematical is a basic tenet. Our activity might have to function in terms of a massive *indexicality,* aphilosophically. This would require epistemic organisation, revision etc. Considering sets of interrelated items may lead to progress towards finding out what instrumentalities our teleological priorities commit us to.

Much of the activity has been involved in self-description; indeed, a form of "self-description-trying." A basis might be: if we describe whatever it is we are doing, how does that description alter what we are doing? There are of course no neutral descriptions, any description is relative to one point of view. Slogans: (i) "Analytic" 1969–70, (ii) "Theory-trying" 1971–72, (iii) "Talking to each other" 1972–73. (There was a sense in each of these of finding out what that particular

> description *committed* us to.) But our work doesn't *state* an ideology, it *shows* one (or several).
>
> [We] are concerned with pragmatics. That is, with problems, not idealist "good ideas" (like the past six years of Konzept Kunst), nor with realist "things in the world" (stuff like art objects). The latter enter into the A&L problematic but only in a secondary way. . . . Giving primacy to problems links with our ideology, not our ontology. Thus (citing Hintikka correcting Quine in *Reference and Modality*, p. 153) we have to distinguish between what we are committed to in the sense that we believe it to exist in the world or in some other possible world, and what we are committed to as part of our ways of dealing with the world conceptually, as part of our conceptual system. The former constitute our ontology, the latter our "ideology."[8]

The current interest in A&L that turns on problems of intersubjectivity within the conversations is of little interest to at least two members: Joseph Kosuth and David Bainbridge. They would also, perhaps, find my formulation of the A&L point of view not merely inadequately descriptive of the thrust of their work, but also incapable of including their work. However, their anomalousness to the current range of A&L self-descriptions hardly rules them out of A&L altogether (although Bainbridge, as a matter of fact, recently chose to leave the group), for part of the dynamic of the group depends on the diversity of outlook of its members.

Nor is the concern with intersubjectivity a retreat into the hermetic. All members of A&L accept the obligation to publicness:

> We are not simply concerned with the simplistic idea of solving some of the problems of inter-subjectivity. There is the priority of making public—demonstrating the publicity of—the difficulties of talking to one another. The public paradigm and the repudiation of "private languages" is basic and central as a methodological thesis of the Art & Language Institute.[9]

The hoped-for public is something like "the general (intelligent) reading public"—a reality to at least certain publishers. In practice, however,

ALTERNATE MAP FOR DOCUMENTA (BASED ON CITATION A)

KEY TO MAP

'+' AT THE ORIGIN OF A VERTICAL/HORIZONTAL AXIS INDICATES A COMPATIBILITY BETWEEN THE RELEVANT DOCUMENTS CITED IN THE LEFT-HAND COLUMN AND ON THE TOP ROW OF THE MATRIX;

'—' INDICATES AN INCOMPATIBILITY;

'T' INDICATES THAT THE RELEVANT DOCUMENTS DO NOT SHARE THE SAME LOGICAL/ETHICAL SPACE.

TERRY ATKINSON/DAVID BAINBRIDGE
IAN BURN/MICHAEL BALDWIN
CHARLES HARRISON/HAROLD HURRELL
JOSEPH KOSUTH/MEL RAMSDEN

THE ART & LANGUAGE INSTITUTE
PAUL MAENZ/KÖLN/JUNI 15

Art & Language, Index 01, 1972. *Poster.*

the immediate audience for A&L work lies in the art world. And most of the controversy surrounding A&L arises from its deliberate refusal to satisfy the requirements which this audience, including fellow artists, demands of any art. It is here that a series of crucial problems arises.

Obviously, given the nature of the A&L inquiry, such demands are unrealistic and impossible. When members of A&L review the work of other artists, it is usually in an effort to define oneself by contrast, to see what it is that one refuses to do. But there is also an implicit (sometimes explicit) attempt to change the ideologies of other artists. The tensions which occur in this situation, it appears, result from the incommensurability of the A&L point of view with the formalist, romantic, materialist theory-sets discussed above. For most of the debate the parties "talk through" each other, even at those rare moments when they might seem to be agreeing. The A&L inquiry does not differ from, say, the formalist theory-set in the same way that, say, Einstein's physics differed from Newton's. The latter seem to have some bases in common, making comparison possible (although if Kuhn is right, only seemingly, because both "paradigms" construe these bases differently and both are of sufficient magnitude to determine what such bases of comparison would be). There is no common measure between A&L and formalism because A&L is not a "deep" concept of art, nor are the theories about art which it examines and proposes definitive of it. What happens, rather, is that members of A&L address themselves to theoretical questions current in art-world debate from a point of view developed within an inquiry which, as I've shown, ranges far beyond art questions.

This dialogue takes some very odd forms. Rational argument is threatened by the fact that what counts as "rational" is determined by one's point of view, one's commitment. The available forms of exchange seem to be either the exertion of various psychological pressures, or the elaboration of one's point of view until the other party, for reasons best known to himself, finally concedes its viability. More drastically, there is a sense in which it is impossible to fully understand a particular point of view without adopting it. This has been my experience with the A&L point of view, and it remains the cause of acute frustration to sympathetic critics of A&L. It follows that external conceptions of A&L cannot but be *mis*conceptions. And that, as they say, would seem to be that.[10]

But the discussion won't close itself down so easily. What seems, from my point of view, to be a misconception may well satisfy you as being accurate from your point of view. That is, if we both give up the prospect of persuading each other, we might still be able to refine our differing points of view by further discussion. Yet I am unwilling to settle for so little rationality. Having offered so far an outline of my own views of the present state of art, and a general account of what I take to be the A&L point of view, I want now to give some reasons why I consider the many versions of A&L currently abroad in the art world to be mistaken, incomplete, or irrelevant. While full understanding of another's point of view is impossible externally, it *is* possible to understand more or less adequately the notion that there is an A&L point of view in art contexts, and that it has certain characteristic assumptions and modes of operation. To believe that "Art & Language" is an art movement would be a misunderstanding of this sort.

There is a further basic cause of the current misconceptions of A&L. The outline of the A&L point of view introduced here will be unrecognizable to many people because it does not seem to encompass the A&L work they know. It might be asked: Why have I said little of the essays in early issues of *Art-Language*? What of the many exhibitions in galleries in England, Europe, and, less often, in New York? What of the "early work" of Atkinson, Baldwin, Burn, Kosuth, Ramsden, etc., so much a part of Conceptual Art in the mid- and late 1960s? These questions perhaps occur because of a failure to notice the shifts in intuitions as to possibilities for inquiry that happened within A&L first in late 1968, early 1969, and again during 1971 and 1972. These shifts were to the point of view upon which I have concentrated so far; they were *from* an A&L which might be better known.

In A&L self-conceptions, there is no underplaying that the first glimpses of a possible inquiry of some interest were formed in the crucible of British philosophy of language and the mid-1960s immediate post-Minimal art context. There are no apologies for this not having been a "clean and easy birth." Nor is there any current feeling of obligation to past failures, or successes. For the ongoing A&L discourse the import of one's history is only its usefulness for the ongoingness of that discourse as of now; however, this is by definition no answer to those external to A&L. So let's see what answers can be given.

A&L is visual art in the forms of writing/words/text/book.

This view is based on two mistaken assumptions: that A&L's typical mode of presentation is typed words on sheets of paper arranged along a gallery wall, and that this mode is somehow essential to the "meaning" of the essays so presented. The truth is that articles in journals, lectures, seminars, and above all conversations, are the typical presentational modes of A&L work, and that while gallery displays are "baggage" unavoidable in the art context within which A&L *partially* operates, they are incidental to what is being said in the essays, etc. To persist in the belief that this criticism of A&L counts is to fail to see past the fallacy that innovation in art takes place primarily (if not essentially) in terms of morphological change. Some have even used this contention in an effort to reduce the whole A&L enterprise to an avant-gardist ploy of questioning the nature of art by (trivial) innovations in the use of materials.[11] This is as mistaken antipathetically as the odd idea of "book as artwork" is mistaken sympathetically in relation to A&L.[12]

A slightly more sophisticated misconception along these lines is to regard A&L essays as post-Duchampian Readymades, as qualifying "as art" under the McLuhanesque rubric of "art is whatever you can get away with in the art context." Where this idea does have some bearing, the situation was quite the reverse—one of the first ideas to surprise Atkinson, Bainbridge, Baldwin, and Hurrell in 1966–67 was the question: what is implied when an artwork is taken out of the art context and placed in one where it doesn't function as art? It should be obvious that there are many, much easier ways of doing the simple thing of controversially locating something in the art context than the kind and depth of work that typifies A&L.

When the "irreducible visuality" of visual art is raised against A&L and other nonconforming art, what is perhaps nascent is a rallying to the gates against barbarous threats to the integrity of the category "art." But if the concept of art is consensually an open one, we can't demand that all candidates first qualify under such closed concepts as "painting," "sculpture," etc. So it is at least contentious that "visuality" is a necessary (not to say sufficient) condition of something's being art.

Others might want to argue, not from necessary qualities (properties) but from definitional cases. That is, visual art should properly approximate its indisputable artworks, literary art its exemplary instances, and so on. Synthetic or hybrid forms are permissible, on this view, but they are importantly components of already constituted categories. In this light A&L becomes hybrid visual art, literature, philosophy, etc.

As Wartofsky has noted, when we are caught in a categorical ambiguity, we have three possible courses of action: to resolve the ambiguity by incorporating the problematic case into our habitual canon; to revise our canon radically, perhaps to the point of replacing it; or to leave the ambiguity unresolved and manipulate very different and perhaps mutually exclusive canons at will or as the occasion demands. He calls these options "conservative," "radical," and "opportunistic," respectively. It should be clear by now that the first and second are not readily available with regard to A&L. As he goes on to say:

> Anti-art, non-art, end-of-art are claims not so much against art, but against the category within which art is framed; that is, they are not so much demands for an end to categorization, as for an end to a specific categorization, and for a recategorization.[13]

A&L members are not indifferent to the incessant recategorizing epidemic in art talk, but it is hard to imagine just what a recategorization which included A&L would be like. So, at most, A&L has an "opportunist" position on this question.

The "art" in A&L writings lies in the style in which they are written. This is an extension of the above misconception—a shift from how the work is displayed to the manner in which it is written/spoken, while still avoiding *what* is said. To Lippard "words, thoughts, tortuous systems are their *material*" while Collins ridicules what he calls "Joycean prose" and "intellectual collaging," as if A&L members willfully sought out recondite philosophical exotica, rendered it meaningless, then presented their lists according to some hermetic principle—or (dreadful thought!) according to no aesthetic principles at all.[14]

Collins's criticisms are reminiscent of the famous misdescription "explosion in a shingle mill," as applied by Julian Street to Duchamp's *Nude Descending a Staircase* and by Howard Devree to Pollock's method; all three utterly fail to grasp the ordering principles operative in the work.[15] Insofar as there are similarities in the manners in which A&L texts are written, it is simply because the authors are, in the first instance, trying to communicate with each other—they are in constant and close conversation, share many of the same attitudes, read many of the same books, etc. One of these attitudes is an ambivalent skepticism toward all "given" forms and methodologies, *as well as* one's own. So it is hardly surprising that the clarity of expression which follows from even relative certainty as to one's aims and traditions is absent. The obligation to publicness does not extend to adopting the "style" of appearing more certain than one is of what one is saying—as scientists, for example, tend to do.[16] A&L conversations do cover complex, difficult, often intractable subjects—surely no one wants to claim that broad public comprehensibility is the measure of the validity of any statement, in art contexts or out.

The question really is this simple. While one can hardly avoid dealing with the "aesthetics" of one's mode of presentation, to regard such "noise" as *the* "message" of the whole of an A&L information display is myopic distortion. It is really to demand that a quality of "artness," susceptible of "aesthetic contemplation," must be central to any situation which claims to have a bearing on art. This is not an argument, but an exhortation to A&L members to subscribe to a notion of the autonomy of art which they have frequently attacked. This fallacy compromises Bruce Boice's more sympathetic complaint: "Their sentences tend more towards being models for questions of theories of meaning (as Russell's syntactically correct but meaningless sentence is such a model) than being sentences capable of setting forth and examining any such theories."[17]

A&L in relation to philosophy.

For example, Boice sees A&L's "basic aims" as "presenting some sort of philosophical analysis of art theories and art questions in general." While this was an early aim, it is now an incidental one. Lippard worries about not having feedback on A&L "from the linguistic philosophers they emulate," and amusingly characterizes A&L members as inhabiting "a land of Quine and Rroses."[18] Others are less polite: bad philosophy, comic philosophy, half-dressed aestheticians, artists disporting themselves in foreign fields, irresponsibly ignorant of the rules, etc.

The A&L inquiry is not, has never been, nor ever claimed to have been, a philosophy of any sort. This is not to say that it is independent of philosophical inquiry, but simply to expose the crudity of the sequence: A studying B, and A making use of B, makes A a form of B. Any map of A&L reading over the past six years would have to take Russell, Austin, Wittgenstein, Carnap, Tarski, Quine, Husserl, Frege, Kierkegaard, Kuhn, Feyerabend, Chomsky, Fodor and Katz, Martin, Hintikka, Apostel, and others as major landmarks. But, while A&L members often do use the methodological rules employed by these and other philosophers, they see no reason to slavishly follow the ways these philosophers use the rules, simply because their aims are different. Likewise, they do not feel confined to what most philosophers take to be the *proper scope* of philosophical inquiry. Indeed, the philosophers used by A&L members are often those who are deeply questioning received rules and definitions of "proper scope." Philosophy compromised by assumptions of autonomy is of little interest. One instinct that has persisted from the beginning of A&L has been an urge toward a nonspecialized openness of inquiry. Just this openness is crucial to its reason for being.

A&L as a form of Conceptual Art.
There is no doubt that A&L emerged in the mid- and later 1960s from many of the same impulses as other post-Minimal, "Conceptual" art. The first issue of *Art-Language* (Vol. 1, No. 1, May 1969) bore the subtitle "The journal of conceptual art" (subsequently dropped), contained Sol LeWitt's "Sentences on Conceptual Art," a "Poem-Schema" by Dan Graham, Lawrence Weiner's " Statements," as well as an introduction by Terry Atkinson in which he suggested that "an art form can evolve by taking as a point of initial inquiry the language-use of the art society," language-use in "both plastic art itself and its support languages."[19] He devoted most of the essay to speculating about what would be involved in proposing the essay he was writing for candidature as an artwork.

That artists should want, as an aspect of their activity as artists, to inquire into the language of art discourse and into language itself, were impulses crucial to the genesis of A&L but not unique to Atkinson et al. at this time. More definitive was their coming to see such inquiry as central and, eventually, as exclusive of "normal" art practices and attitudes because the newly acquired vantage point made it inescapably obvious that "normal" art was so contradictory, compromised, and anomalous that any return to it was impossible. The steps toward this vantage point were no more free from compromise, contradiction, and anomaly than any other post-Minimal art in that confused time. But they were steps which eventually led out of at least that set of confusions.

A version of the crudest notion of Conceptual Art, the use of "ideas" as a new material, informed the presentation of pieces of linguistic analysis as art in such works as Atkinson/Baldwin's *French Army* and *Hot/Cold* (1967), Kosuth's *Second Investigation* (1968), Ramsden's *Six Negatives* (1968). The regarding of "support" discussions of such art as art is assumed in, for example, Burn's "Read Premiss" for *Six Negatives* (1969), Atkinson et al., *Lecher System* (1970), Bainbridge's *Notes on M1* (1969). But after this we see the growth of something qualitatively different from these mere "extensions" of normal art practice—we see the growth of the A&L point of view such as I've described, an activity constituting itself as inquiry uncircumscribed by even covert demands that it bear some relation, however indirect, to "art theories and art questions." Of course, the inquiry *may* have such a bearing and often

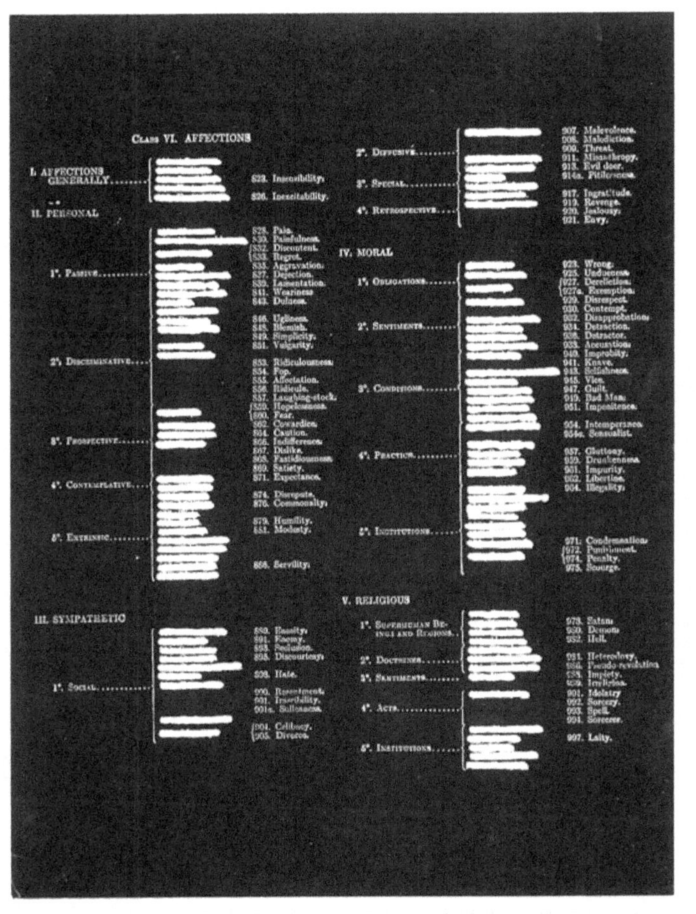

Mel Ramsden, Six Negatives, *1968. Bound book: 14 leaves, 13 photo lithographs.*

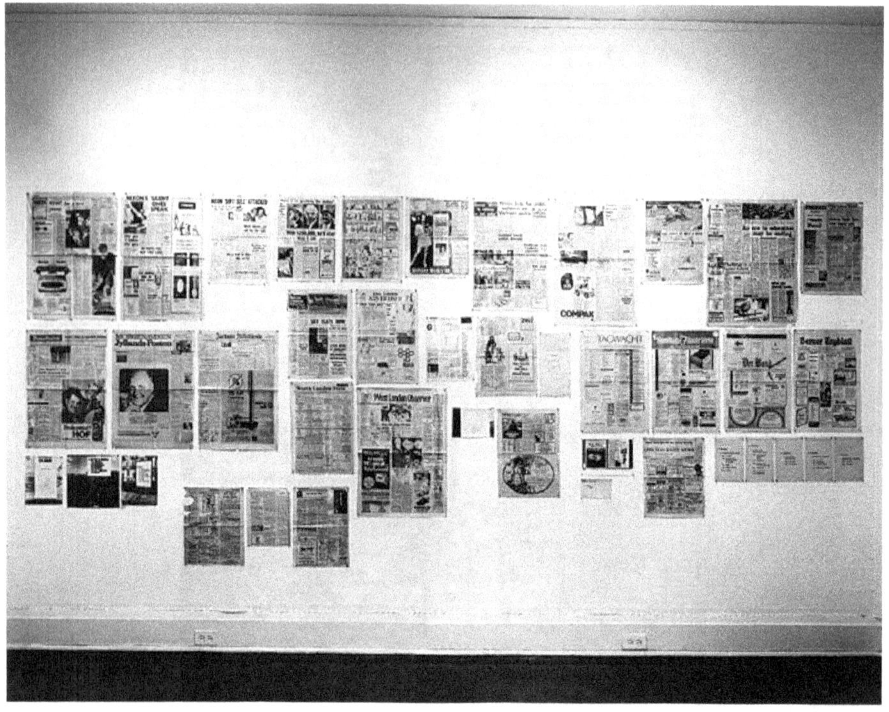

Joseph Kosuth, The Second Investigation, *1968.*
Inserts into newspapers and onto billboards. Installation view,
the Renaissance Society at the University of Chicago, 1976.

does, but such a bearing was no longer definitive nor was it claimed to be an adequate justification of it.

Therefore, developed A&L is different not just in degree but in kind from its "Conceptual Art" origins. Its basic aims, and its methodologies, differ radically from those of Conceptual Art—indeed, of any recognized art. No matter how diverse and seemingly new its aspect, all post-Minimal, Conceptual Art subsists under one or other, or some combination of, those formalist, romantic, or materialist theory-sets which I discussed near the beginning of this essay. Committed as they are to one or another of these theory-sets, critics have failed to see this distinction of kind, and tend to see it as a difference of degree, with the early work foremost in their minds.[20] Like most of the other misconceptions we have reviewed, this is a natural mistake in the context of the hostility, wariness, and/or indifference which surrounds A&L.

NOTES

This chapter was originally published as Terry Smith, "Art and Art and Language," Artforum *12, no. 6 (February 1974): 49–52.*

1. Thomas S. Kuhn, *The Structure of Scientific Revolutions* (Cambridge: Cambridge University Press, 1962; Chicago: University of Chicago Press, 1970). The latter has an important postscript.

2. See W. B. Gallie, "Essentially Contested Concepts," *Proceedings of the Aristotelian Society* 56 (1955–56): 167–98; and Morris Weitz, "Open Concepts," *Revue Internationale de Philosophie* 99/100 (1972): 86–110.

3. For example, Terry Atkinson, "From an Art & Language Point of View," *Art-Language* 2, no. 2 (February 1970): 25–60; Joseph Kosuth, "Art after Philosophy," *Studio International* (October 1969): 134–37, (November 1969): 160–61, (December 1969): 212–13; Philip Pilkington and David Rushton, *Concerning the Paradigm of Art* (Zürich: Editions Bischofberger, 1970); *Analytical Art* 1 (July 1971).

4. Victor Burgin, "Thanks for the Memory," *Architectural Design* 40 (August 1970): 288–92.

5. Point made by Terry Atkinson and Michael Baldwin, "Some Post-War American Work and Art & Language: Ideological Responsiveness," *Studio International* (April 1972): 164–67.

6. See chapter 2 of Erving Goffman, *The Presentation of Self in Everyday Life* (Garden City, NJ: Doubleday, 1959), 77–105.

7. In England: Terry Atkinson, Michael Baldwin, Charles Harrison, Graham Howard, Howard Hurrell, Phillip Pilkington, and David Rushton. In New York: Ian Burn, Michael Corris, Preston Heller, Joseph Kosuth, Michael Krugman, Andrew Menard, Mel Ramsden, and Terry Smith.

8. Respectively, Baldwin, Burn, Ramsden, early 1973.

9. *The Art & Language Institute: Suggestions for a Map*, Documenta 5 catalog (Kassel, 1972).

10. These remarks attempt to deal with comments made by Lynda Morris after an early version of this essay was given as a lecture to the Royal College of Art, London, June 7, 1973. They are based on Wittgenstein, for example, his *Lectures and Conversations on Aesthetics, Psychology and Religious Belief*, ed. C. Barrett (Oxford: Blackwell, 1966); Kuhn, *Structure of Scientific Revolutions*; Paul K. Feyerabend, "Against Method: Outline of an Anarchistic Theory of Knowledge," *Minnesota Studies in the Philosophy of Science* (1970): 17–130; essays by Popper, Masterman, Feyerabend, Lakatos, and Kuhn in Imre Lakatos and Alan Musgrave, eds., *Criticism and the Growth of Knowledge* (Cambridge: Cambridge University Press, 1970); and others. See important objections in Roger Trigg, *Reason and Commitment* (Cambridge: Cambridge University Press, 1973).

11. For example, James Collins, "Things and Theories," *Artforum* (May 1973): 32–36.

12. Germano Celant, *Book as Artwork* (London: Nigel Greenwood, 1973).

13. Marx W. Wartofsky, "Art, Action and Ambiguity," *Monist* 8, no. 2 (April 1974): 327–38. The idea of "opportunism" in this sort of context is extensively explored in Ian Burn and Mel Ramsden, eds., *A Dithering Device* (Nova Scotia School of Art and Design, 1973). [Editor's note: The latter publication does not exist. *A Dithering Device* is the title of an unpublished manuscript by Burn and Ramsden that has been exhibited on occasion as an artwork. Art & Language did however draw on the concept of opportunism while creating the collective work published as Art & Language, *Blurting in A&L* (New York and Halifax: Art & Language Press and Nova Scotia College of Art, 1973).]

14. See Lucy R. Lippard, ed., *Six Years: The Dematerialization of the Art Object* (New York: Praeger, 1973), 151; and Collins, "Things and Theories," 35.

15. Howard Devree, "Among the New Exhibitions," *New York Times*, March 25, 1945, section 2, page 8.

16. See especially chapter 3 of John Ziman, *Public Knowledge: The Social Dimension of Science* (Cambridge: Cambridge University Press, 1968), 30–62.

17. "Bruce Boice on *Art & Language*," *Artforum* (March 1973): 86.

18. Lippard, *Six Years*, 263, 151.

19. [Terry Atkinson], "Introduction," *Art-Language* 1, no. 1 (May 1969): 8.

20. For example, Lizzie Borden, "Three Modes of Conceptual Art," *Artforum* (June 1972): 68–71; Max Kozloff, "The Trouble with Art-as-Idea," *Artforum* (September 1972): 33–37; Carter Ratcliff, "Notes on the Future of an Esthetic," *Art International* (November 1972): 70–74, 95, 100.

ART
&
LANGUAGE

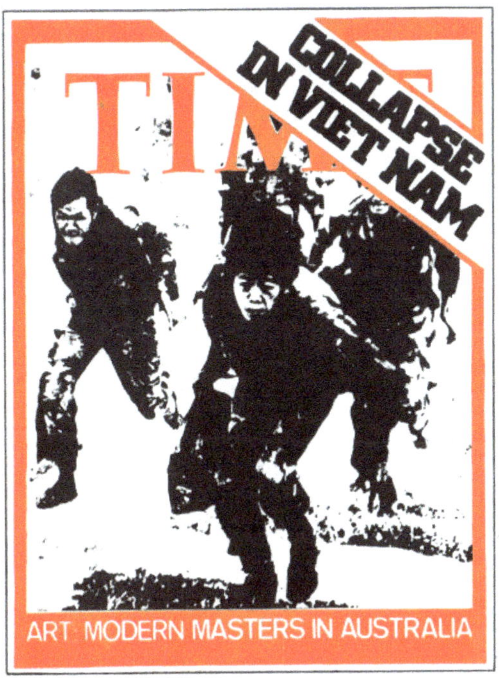

1975 $5

Terry Smith, ed., Art & Language: Australia 1975, *cover. Sydney, Banbury, New York: Art & Language Press, 1976.*

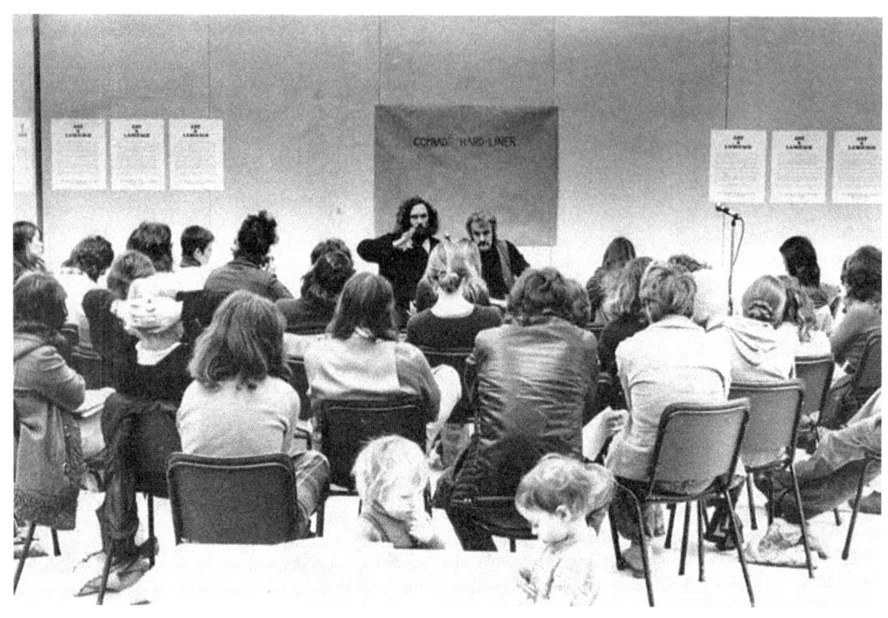

Art & Language, Art & Language, *Art Gallery of South Australia, Adelaide, 1975, discussion (Terry Smith and Noel Sheridan).*

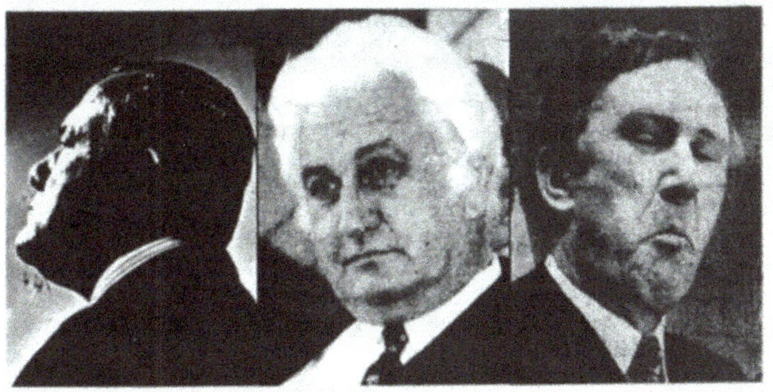

Art & Language (P), Art & Language, *Auckland City Art Gallery, Auckland, 1976. Poster, 570 × 450 mm, designed with assistance of Chips Mackinolty and printed by him.*

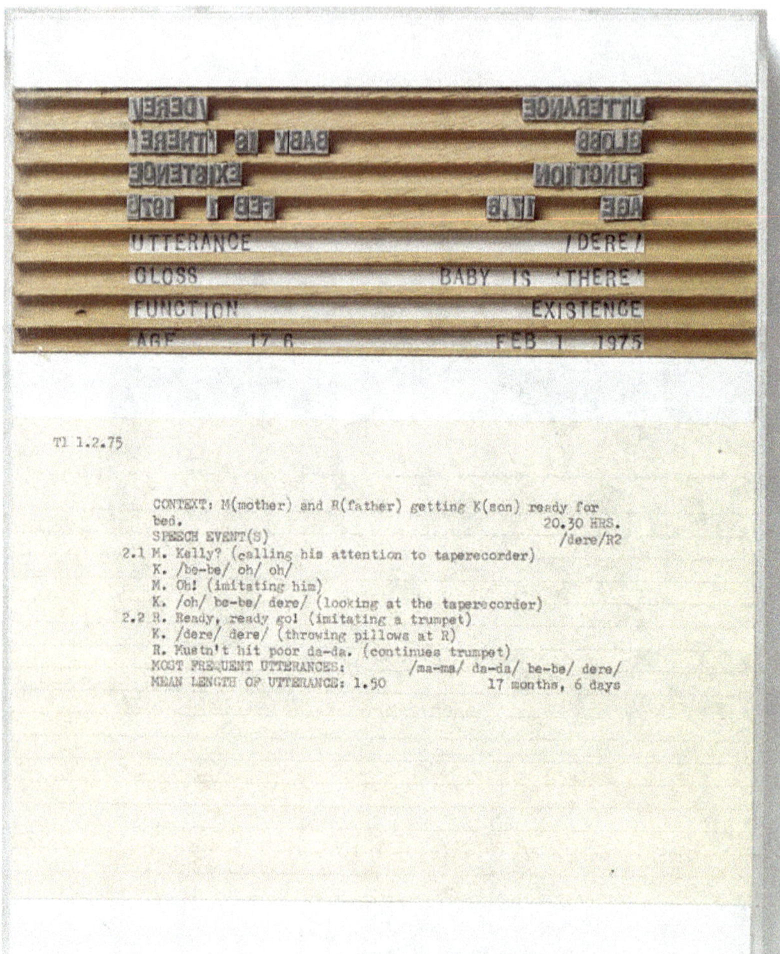

Mary Kelly, The Post-Partum Document, *1973–79,* Documentation II: Analysed Utterances and Related Speech Events, *1975 (detail). Perspex unit, white card, sugar paper, crayon. 1 of 13 units, 28.5 × 36.5 cm each. Art Gallery of Ontario © the artist.*

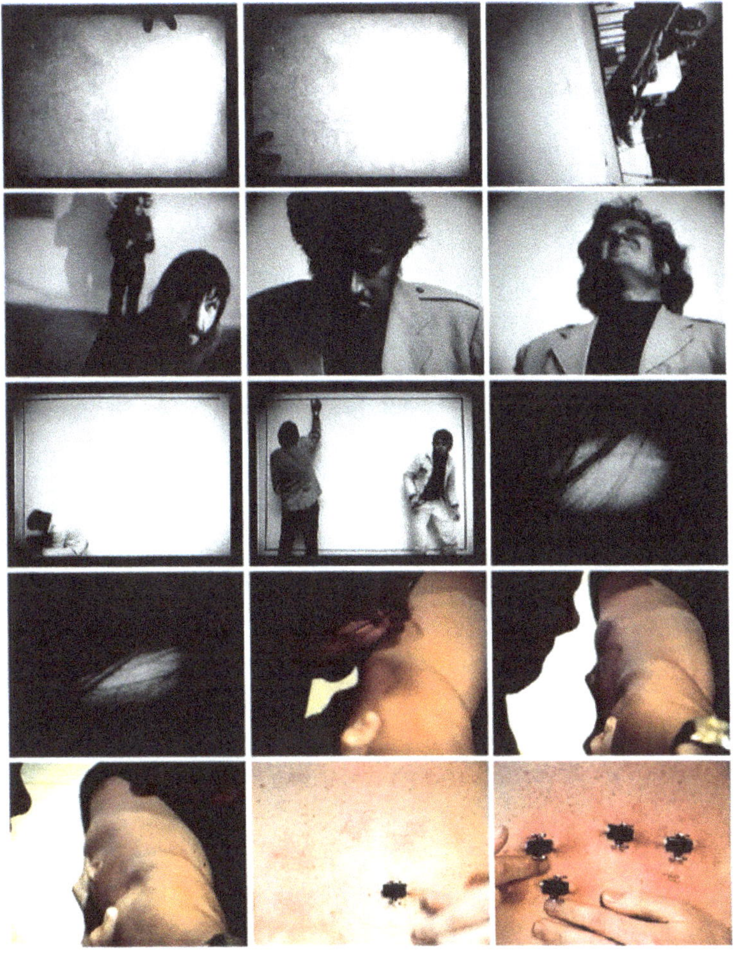

Mike Parr and Peter Kennedy, Idea Demonstrations, *1972. 16mm film, 40 min., black and white and color, optical sound. Collection of the artists.*

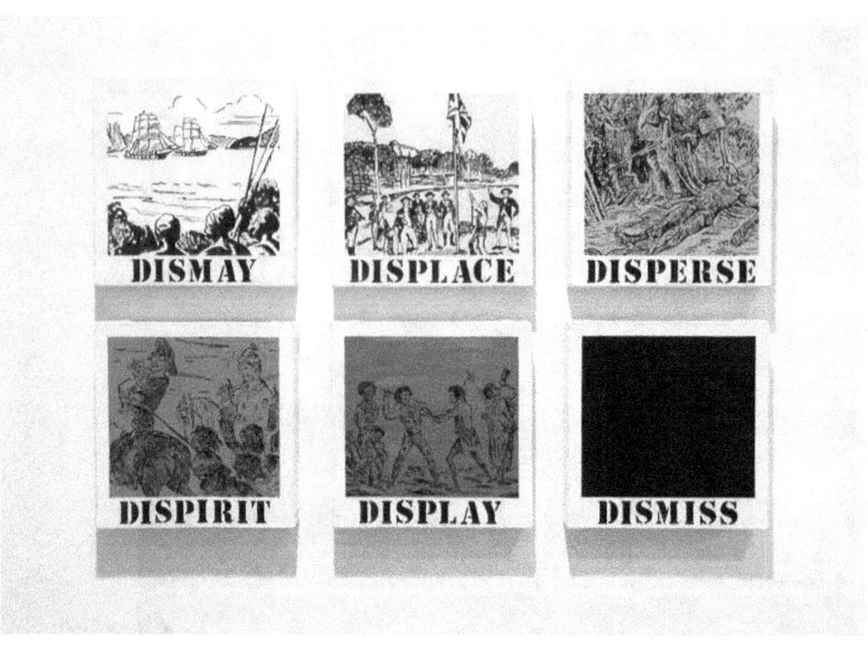

Gordon Bennett, Untitled *(dismay, displace, disperse, dispirit, display, dismiss), 1989. Oil and synthetic polymer paint on canvas, Museum of Contemporary Art, gift of Doug Hall, 1993. Image courtesy Museum of Contemporary Art Australia © Gordon Bennett Estate 2015.*

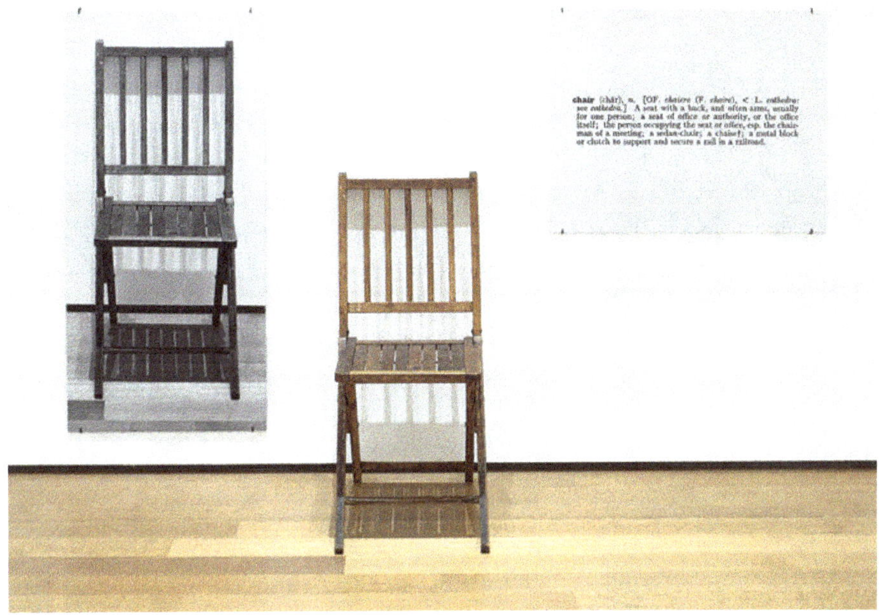

Joseph Kosuth, One and Three Chairs, *1965. Museum of Modern Art, New York. © 2015 Joseph Kosuth / Artists Rights Society (ARS), New York.*

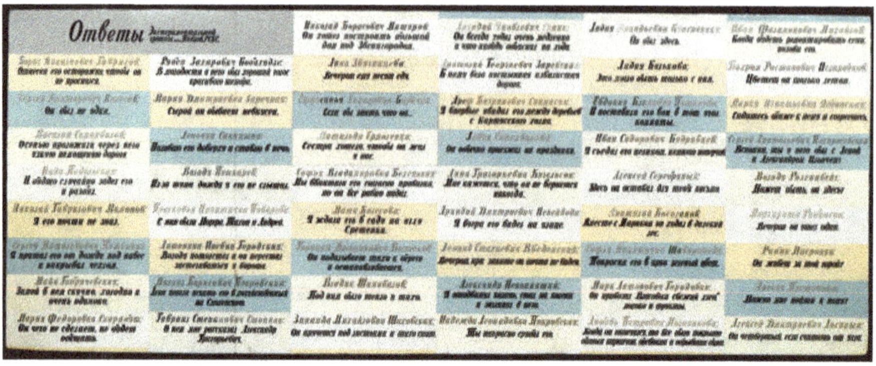

Ilya Kabakov, Answers of the Experimental Group, *1970–71. Orgalit, enamel. 147 × 376 cm © 2015 Artists Rights Society (ARS), New York / VG Bild-Kunst, Bonn.*

The Tasks of Translation 2

Art & Language in Australia and New Zealand 1975–76

It is now recognized that the politics of provincialism preoccupied artists everywhere in the mid-1970s. Geographic and, more importantly, cultural distance from dominant metropolitan centers such as New York, and from the new network emerging in Europe, particularly in Italy and Germany, were acutely experienced. The power to confer recognition and reward, but above all the power to set the agenda of what counted as significant art and criticism, seemed to be sourced forever elsewhere. Deep resentment was felt by those working in the so-called centers yet marginalized by the Modernist orthodoxies prevailing there—felt, that is, by women artists, and by those from racial and ethnic minorities. Just as strong were the feelings of artists living in the cultural peripheries, in the dependent worlds of the old colonies and the newly emerging economies. From these places, and from the dispossessed artists of the First World, came the sharpest critiques of the institutionalization of the avant-garde, as well as the extremes of formal experimentation, the bizarre hybrids, the insistence on difficult content, the radical searching for new audiences. This anti-Modernism was, in my view, just as strong an impulse of the mid- and later 1970s as were the apolitical ironies, which captured (however briefly) the catchy appellation "postmodernism." It may, in the long run, turn out to have been the most inventive and effective current. I believe that it was, in our region at least. If this proves to be so, our conceptions of recent art history need much rewriting.

While these larger currents are matters of frequent debate, what tend to be overlooked are the specific ways in which the big issues have their impacts. It was no coincidence that, in the early 1970s, conceptual artists, particularly those interested in languages and their operations, raised the political questions first, often even obsessively. Nor was it mere chance that they saw questions of power as issues at all levels, both macro and micro. Questions of meaning preoccupied them, including questions as to the nature and even the possibility of meaning. It is scarcely surprising, then, that the tribulations of trying to translate between languages—especially artistic ones—were where the problems of difference and incommensurability hit home sharply, at the fundamental creative and interpretative drives.

My basic proposition is that the demands of the mid-1970s moment created a new role for certain artists, and for newly empowered art audiences: that of *translator*. Or, more accurately, a fresh inflexion of an old activity became pressing: individual translations between items of other visual cultures took on, for many artists and audiences, a much more activist, public dimension. We became translators between competing contemporary cultures. How some of us fared in these circumstances may have some historical interest. More importantly, the ideas of the artist as translator and of the audience as creative readers are regaining current relevance, as cultures split, splice, and splinter again with a rapidity even greater than fifteen years ago.

OF TRANSLATABILITY

Around 1970, the classic text on the theory of translation was Walter Benjamin's "The Task of the Translator," the introduction to his 1923 rendering of Baudelaire's *Tableaux Parisiens*.[1] He argued that translation was not ruled by accuracy, was not usefully understood as a warring between fidelity and license, and was barbarous when it became a literal rendering from language to language. Translation, rather, made possible the "afterlife" of original texts, occurring when both languages concerned had evolved beyond the moment of the original writing. It was a mode of releasing the translatability of the original, its potentiality for change, for becoming literature—or, in his words, for realizing a text's capacity to become "pure language," transcending that in which it was written. It follows that good translation does not shift a text from one language to another; instead it enriches the translator's language by importing the purity of the text being translated, by enabling that text to echo within the translator's language in ways parallel to its original effects in its own language. Good translation, therefore, is untranslatable.

Benjamin went on to speak of the "kinship of languages" on this elevated level, one that enabled the "fulfillment" of languages, thereby "integrating the tongues." He cited Mallarmé:

> The imperfection of languages consists in their plurality, the supreme one is lacking: thinking is writing without accessories or even whispering, the immortal word still remains silent; the diversity of idioms on earth prevents everybody from uttering the words which otherwise, at a single stroke, would materialise as truth.

Writing of this nature, including translation, was the "language of truth." He acknowledged, on the other hand, the "essential foreignness of languages," and that translation was a mode of "provisionality" in relation to this incommensurability. But he concluded by stressing the thirst of writing, again including translation, to reach beyond this toward a total unity of signification, content, and reality. Thus all language aspires to the condition of Holy Writ, revelation being the only condition under which unity is achievable. This celebration of Scripture as the ultimate writing seemed bizarre to those of us then reading Benjamin for his tangential takes on historical materialism. Like the assumption throughout the essay that it is great art that most calls for translation, such mysticism seemed an eccentric aberration, an echo of his Talmudic past, best edited out, like the odd bits about the "aura" of original artworks in his "The Work of Art in the Age of Mechanical Reproduction," read ragged at the time for its proposals about political effectivity in art.[2]

The question of translation was also present at the "birth" of deconstruction, its emergence from formal semiology. In a 1967 interview Jacques Derrida echoed Benjamin remarkably closely:

> Within the limits of its possibility, or its *apparent* possibility, translation practices the difference between signified and signifier. But, if this difference is never pure, translation is even less so, and a notion of *transformation* must be substituted for the notion of translation: a regulated transformation of one language by another, one text by another. We shall not have and never have had to deal with some "transfer" of pure signifieds that the signifying instrument—or "vehicle"—would leave virgin and intact, from one language to another, or within one and the same language.[3]

Derrida is, however, attempting something that Benjamin dealt with in other ways: he is beginning to wreak havoc upon the Saussurian concept of the sign as consisting in a signifier (a sensible part, such as a sound, word, or image) and a signified (an intelligible part, such as a concept, referent, or meaning), particularly the expectation that the former gives systematic access to the latter. Indeed, he sees these two parts as essentially in opposition, just as they are always imbricated in, and contaminated by, each other. His remarks about translation occur within a broader discussion about how metaphysics (to him, most philosophy) imposes on semiology, the science of signs, a never-ending search for a "transcendental signified," that is, a concept independent of language. God is the most obvious example of such a concept; and it is easy to see how it follows, as Benjamin concluded, that Holy Writ would then be both the beginning and the end of all language-use, existing at a point both before and after translation.

But this opposition between semiology and metaphysics, between language and a transcendent concept, itself has the form of a conflict between signifier and signified. This is, I believe, what Derrida is getting at in the following remarks, which immediately precede the passage cited above:

> That this opposition cannot be radical or absolute does not prevent it from functioning, and even from being indispensable within certain limits—very wide limits. For example, no translation would be possible without it. And in fact the theme of a transcendental signified was constituted within the horizon of an absolutely pure, transparent and unequivocal translatability.[4]

Benjamin—and Mallarmé—would have recognized, and concurred, with these themes: no conflict between signifier and signified means a closed language world, with no space, need, or possibility of translation, whereas conflict between the worlds of the languages provokes the desire for a space beyond them, one where they might all be translated into pure language, into writing itself, *écriture*.

Yet, while Derrida is summarizing his predecessors, he is also driving into new readings. Two key words mark out the shifts. He speaks of translation "practicing" the difference between signifier and signified; that is, the preferred relationship here is one of rehearsal, testing, learning, and trying out possibilities rather than a mechanical reproduction of fixed difference. More importantly, he substitutes transformation for translation, recognizing the impossibility of clean transposition, of simple "transfer" from one language to another. Certainly, at this stage, it is a "regulated" exchange, yet, as Derrida's deconstructive enterprise expanded, regularities became obstacles quickly overcome in the search for the irregular, for traces, marginalities, differences, for *différance* itself.

The problematics of translation pervade Derrida's writings. They provide many typical deconstructive strategies: for example, the re-reading of Plato's *Phaedrus* via its mistranslations.[5] Deconstruction typically presumes the predominance of the signifier, the priority of regimes of signs, their intertextuality. Is not translation a kind of intertextuality—indeed, is it not the writing practice most committed to the interaction of texts? Is not the figure most privileged by deconstruction—the reader who reads against the grain of the text—a translator of the kind celebrated by Benjamin and Derrida, that is, a *transformer?* Finally, is not this translator/transformer one of the most striking personifications of that very same reader whose birth from the ashes of "the death of the author" was being so eloquently celebrated at the time by Barthes and Foucault?[6] Does it not follow that translation becomes itself a transformatory *practice,* no longer secondary and dependent on "original" texts, but as primary as other forms of writing, as embedded in the intertextuality of all writing as they are?

Derrida was scarcely known to English-speaking artists in the late 1960s/early 1970s, despite the impact of his work in French intellectual circles. Barthes was known, Foucault becoming so. Yet many of these themes emerge in Conceptual Art of the period, especially that concerned with theorizing the new prominence of the spectator and the changing relations between art and language.

LANGUAGE AND ART: LATE 1960S/EARLY 1970S

Despite the markedly international character of Conceptual Art, and the widespread—at times, dominant—interest in language among most of the artists involved, translation is rarely articulated as a major concern during the early years. I can find no reference to it in any of the thousands of pieces, projects, texts, actions, and publications from the period 1966 to 1972 collated by Lucy Lippard in her anthology *Six Years*.[7] Ian Burn and Mel Ramsden's *Soft-Tape* (1966) is an exception: devised in London for an exhibition in Melbourne that did not take place, it consisted of a tape-recorder on a pedestal in an otherwise empty room, playing a spoken text at an audibility level just below the sound of sense. In his notes on the re-creation of this piece for the 1990 Sydney Biennale, Ian Burn recalls: "Communication, we argued, isn't just a semantic or conceptual problem of translation (deducing the 'right' correspondences and so on) but is also crucially a spatial problem. . . . If the semantic uncertainty is inseparable from spatial considerations, then the spectator not only is the translator but also becomes the measurement of the space." This format would appear, in dramatically different circumstances, in the Art & Language exhibitions in Australia in 1975.

Almost all Conceptual Art involves language, most minimally in explanatory notes to documentations of actions, events, or processes; most completely when language-use is taken as the paradigm human activity and concern with exploring its structures becomes paramount. How could translation be a nonissue in such contexts? How could such intellectually alert people treat translation as if it were transparent? Three reasons suggest themselves: internationalism, art's autonomy, and the dominance of formal theories of language.

Internationalism in art is never neutral. With the disintegration of New York as the pace-setting, global art making, and marketing center in the years around 1970, two quite contrary tendencies began to flower in the resultant vacuum. One was a regionalist revaluation of local histories and initiatives—of which more later. The other was the sudden sense that the next avant-garde innovations could come from anywhere: experimental work from Toronto, London, Cologne, Milan, Sarajevo, San Francisco, Sydney, and elsewhere began to appear in new magazines, in photocopied catalogs, and in exchanges through the mails. The model here was antithetical to the cultural imperialism of the New York–based Modernist Machine, imposing its structures and values on its artistic colonies. It was more that of the randomizing, argumentative celebration of disruptive difference that marked the excentricity of the Dadaists, the Surrealists, and, most recently, the Fluxus groups. An international community of artists quickly developed, based on direct contact, indirect information, and the creation of new forms of publicity, such as Seth Siegelaub's *March 1–31, 1969*, the first catalog-only exhibition. At this stage, much conceptual work existed most significantly in reproduced form. The language of its reproduction tended to be that of its publisher or distributor, that is, English and, to a lesser extent, German. An alternative, but still avant-gardist, internationalism was evolving (one that the gallery system, soon to regroup its forces, would find helpful when it came to picking out the new generation of promotable artists). While issues of translation frequently came up as practical problems in the course of the day-to-day organization of this network (three pieces of mine are still somewhere in Italy), they rarely surfaced as in themselves the source of a creative problematic. The alternative internationalism, at this stage, meant solidarity against the Modernist academy rather than divisiveness based on national or personal differences. A common enemy obviated individual acrimony, as did the desire for collaborative modes of working. In Derrida's terms, you could say that both acted as "transcendental signifieds," making translation unnecessary.

Assumptions about the autonomy of art also had their impact. As noted before, many artists sought spaces for invention beyond the atrophied history of Modernist orthodoxy, represented above all by hard-edge and colorfield painting, by painted metal sculpture, and by formalist art criticism. Formalist artists and critics made claims for art's essential separateness as totalizing as any that had been made before.[8] Some conceptual artists, in the early years, were just as vehement that art should be about art before anything else, and that it be made for artists before all others. Joseph Kosuth's influential essay "Art after Philosophy" is typical of this mood.[9] But this kind of autonomy and reflexivity had, in the most innovative work, a quite distinct inflexion. While formalists celebrated art's autonomy as fundamental to conserving its quality and its continuity, conceptual artists, convinced that art as it has evolved was irredeemable, saw reflexivity as the first step toward the possibility of radically reconceiving art altogether. Painting, sculpture, all the traditional modes of image-making, were exhausted. For a time, mixed media seemed the way to go, but it lacked clarity for many. The creation of objects invited their instant commoditization by a vast, voracious, and increasingly desperate art marketing system. Even the seemingly neutral presumption that visual art be in some sense visual became subject to extensive controversy. For some artists, each of these problems seemed merely issues within a larger, more terminally threatening dilemma. Art itself was at stake, not just its media, its forms, its secondary languages, its contexts, audiences, and institutions. The concept of Art was up for grabs.

The maneuver here can again be put in terms of Derrida's earlier distinction. Taking normal art practice as a semiotic one (as a system for the production and reproduction of signifiers), its failure in the years around 1970 to transform the babble of its languages into a viable, continuing art, obliged metaphysics to impose on it the task of re-examining its roots. Given the eternal conflict between signifier and signified, this can only be done through the domination (however temporary) of a signified—in this case, the concept of Art itself; the previous transcendental signifier, Modernism, having so conspicuously collapsed. Left as a domain of simple sign-production (a world of signifiers), art making is condemned to incessant repetition, to closure, to impossibility, to say nothing of untranslatability. Thus the invasion of a transcendental signified, thus the necessity for reflexivity.

The most radical Conceptual Art was radical because it unequivocally seized the task of going directly to these roots. It assumed that the concept of Art existed most fundamentally not in "the mind," nor in works of art (be they great or the whole class), but in language. There were other quite influential ideas around: Richard Wollheim, for example, argued that Art was "the institution of art," that is, all the beliefs, practices, relationships, and organizations that surrounded and constituted the production of art objects.[10] Language was relevant, in that Wollheim, like many others including Donald Brook in Australia, held that art objects, practices, etc., were such because they were usually identified as such by the words and the actions of those in the relevant community. Art was what people normally said it was, and borderline cases could be settled in the usual way, by disputations and the evolution of customary acceptance or rejection. The idea of institution here is an analogy to ordinary language-use.

Wittgenstein's influence also pervades the early interests of English conceptualists such as Art & Language. Terry Atkinson opened the editorial in the first issue of *Art-Language* (May 1969) with the hypothesis that "this editorial, in itself an attempt to evince some outlines as to what 'conceptual art' is, is held out as a 'conceptual art' work." This attracted much more attention—being a striking, avant-gardist ambit claim—than the substantive content of his piece, the proposal for how to go on as artists in the impasse: "I would suggest that it is not beyond the bounds of sense to maintain that an art form can evolve by taking as a point of initial inquiry the language-use of the art society." The rest of the article, and others in the same issue, contained commentary on various earlier projected "artworks," along with notes on their putative viewers, including an alien. In the second issue of *Art-Language* (Feb. 1970), Atkinson's essay "From an Art & Language Point of View" applied this kind of analysis to predecessors such as Duchamp and contemporaries such as Robert Barry. In New York (and, prior to that, London), Ian Burn and Mel Ramsden had independently arrived at a similar set of concerns, and Joseph Kosuth was using information from the investigative sciences in his series of displays entitled *Investigations*. Students at the Coventry School of Art, Philip Pilkington and David Rushton, founded the journal *Analytical Art* (July 1971).

Art & Language writings soon dispensed with physical objects, however conjectural, as beginning-points for inquiry, concentrating on ideas of and about art that were circulating in the international art world, testing them as statements against the group's growing knowledge of linguistic philosophy. By 1971 Art & Language had moved from a phase where it was, like much other Conceptual Art, analytic of art's making and theorization, to a more distinctive set of intentions. These pushed beyond anything that the stylistic category "Conceptual Art" could encompass. They were, as I put it in 1974, "to construct a complex methodology for nonspecialist critical discourse which would function in the 'interstices' between some of the concepts and procedures raised thus far within specialisms such as art, philosophy, sociology, etc."[11] Typical methodological approaches were relativism, "theory-trying," recursivity, and falsification.

Translation was of interest to the logicians, such as Quine, the philosophers of language, such as Goodman and Hintikka, and the logicians of languages such as Apostel and Fodor and Katz. But the overriding concern of these men was the systematic description of the regular behavior of language users, and they typically applied formal logic in generating structures for artificial languages and in accounting for the operations of natural languages. Translation tended to become a readily deferrable problem, probably easily solved, especially in the most formal systems, by some kind of direct transfer. These spaces were, however, elusive and unstable, and approaches to these were tentative, disparate.

But it was the extreme, even absurd, implications of such systematization that attracted artists: a statement about translatability such as Nelson Goodman's "With suitable principles of correlation, Constable's landscape painting could provide an enormous amount of information about a pink elephant" highlighted a freedom of signification that seemed enormously liberating.[12] It also flagged an edge to the academic discipline of linguistic analysis, an excess requiring the intervention of those working in the "interstices" between the specialisms. Inspired also by Kuhn's dramatic theories of science's paradigm shifts, and by Feyerabend's anarchistic epistemology, this was just where Art & Language wanted to be.

It was, however, during the next two phases of Art & Language's development that issues around translation became increasingly important. Art & Language had expanded to two "groups": one based around Banbury and Coventry, the other in New York, with a variable membership of approximately eight each. By 1972–73 communication within and between each group became the overt object of inquiry. Was the constant conversation within Art & Language "a body of discourse that literally just searches," or could the semantics and the ideologies active in the exchanges be mapped in some ways? English members developed an index, a program map, and began compiling an idiolectic dictionary, while the New York group collected its written and verbal "blurts," annotating them with comments from other members, then sought ways to make the conversations accessible to others. Both groups were taking themselves as actual language communities, and exploring their imbrication in whatever might be basic about language structures as well as the much more free-wheeling actualities (the pragmatics) of their language use.

Among the four hundred "blurts" chosen from the annotating project conducted by New York members of Art & Language between January and June 1973 and collected in a *Handbook (Blurting in A&L)*, there are fourteen collated under the heading "Translation."[13] Some were reports on current theories of translation; others commented on the limitations of such theorization. Some reflected concern about acting in the gaps between disciplines; still others indicated anxiety about communication in a divided art world; thus no. 366: "If we (say) want to 'talk to painters' we can't abstract a general theory of painting and then set up a comparison theory between that and our own 'theories.' For the painter (etc.) theoretical implications don't enter a level on which that comparison theory might function. This is the kind of translation problem we can't avoid . . ." Finally, in blurt no. 363, translation was recognized as problematic for the group itself: "If we don't admit some kind of translation problem then we can only talk at each other. Excluding the 'problematic' of translation we will exclude all anomalies, contradictions, baggage, etc. (that is, all the interesting stuff)."

Two issues of *Art-Language* in 1974 were devoted to theorizing the group's particular, and peculiar, sociality, as were many exhibitions in Europe and the United States.[14] In 1975 I characterized this phase as follows:

> In contrast to the personal subjectivity ("I speak with my own voice") which prevails in the artworld, and to the impersonal supra-subjectivity of groups and committees ("We speak with

Blurting in A&L: an index of blurts and their concatenation (the Handbook) constitutes a problematic; that is, you can't (at least not without
deliberation) ignore possible pathways without losing embeddedness
(idiolects); deliberation (here, the issue of going-on becomes a self-
conscious construction for the reader) admits broader reflection of a
context of our/your/other activities: namely, the structure of our/your
language/culture and (the prospect of) revisability of our/your lang-
uage/culture. Published 1973 by Art & Language Press, 250 Bowery.
New York, N.Y. and The Mezzanine, Nova Scotia College of Art, 1875
Granville Street, Halifax, N.S.

Art & Language, Handbook (Blurting in A&L), *cover. New York: Art & Language Press; Halifax: Nova Scotia College of Art and Design, 1973.*

> one voice"), the Art & Language world of discourse searches for a personal intersubjectivity ("I speak with many voices").[15]

Translation, in all its senses, became more and more an issue as communications within Art & Language, and between the group and others in the art world, became increasingly volatile. Art & Language was achieving its maximal impact, but this coincided with accelerating internal conflict, particularly between the English and New York groups, and with the full-scale disintegration of the Modernist Machine as the dominant regulator of international art practice.

AUSTRALIA 1975: IT'S TIME PAST

Nixon's moral bankruptcy had seeped through American society and was intolerably fouling Southeast Asia: he had breached his Watergate. England's decline as a postwar superpower had passed the point of no return: it had become enslaved by "the gnomes of Zurich." And then there were the multiplicity of micro-imperialisms that affected artists as much as anyone else: the hard economics of scraping a living for some but not others, the structural repression of women, the near-invisibility of minority viewpoints. To more and more members of the group it began to seem that the Art & Language point of view was too narrow, and that the searching conversation, despite its increasingly radical form, was shriveling into irrelevance. Translation between different language-worlds was still a pressing problematic, even more so, as it was evident that these worlds were coterminous not only with nations, and with classes and subcultures within them, but also with groupings inside the subcultures, even with individuals. Sociolects became idiolects, ideologies also existed as idiologies.[16]

The same absences mark all the thinking about translation so far discussed: Benjamin's, Derrida's, those of the linguistic philosophers, those in the Art & Language blurts. Social, economic, and cultural inequality haunts translation; it is not an abstract transit lounge, an esperanto of artificial possibility, a direct mapping of one grammar onto another, a conflation of dictionaries. As words, concepts, and images travel from one language world to another they lose as much baggage as they carry. At stake here is not just the "natural wastage" of inevitable cultural difference. In a world where international capitalism relentlessly seeks to impose cultural conformity, yet constantly and conspicuously fails to do so, what are really put at risk are all the universalizing concepts: world

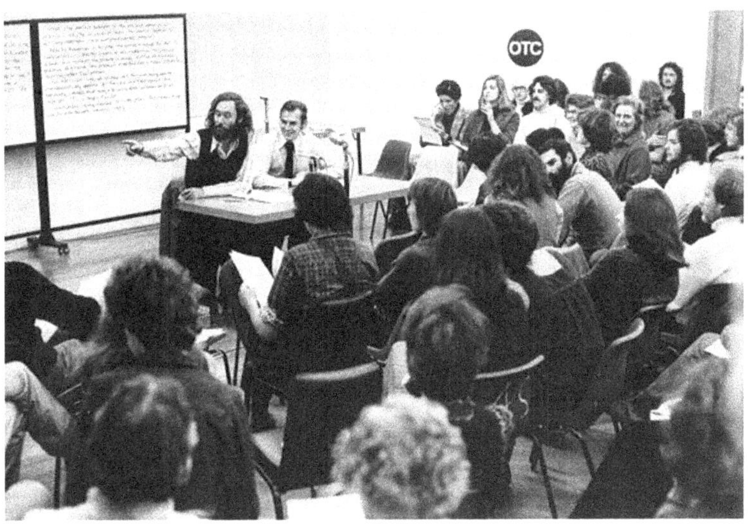

Art & Language, Art & Language, *National Art School, Melbourne, 1975, discussion (Terry Smith and Patrick McCaughey). Photo: Suzanne Davies.*

government, the great historical narratives, a global economy, the very figure of Man, humanism and all its derivatives . . . to say nothing of the canonical achievements of art and literature, the avant-garde adventure of Modernism, or even the day-to-day routines of the international art world. If translation between all human languages is, in principle, possible, if works of art are readable by all, then these hopes and presumptions of modernity are at least grounded in some kind of adequate human communication. If not, then they, too, are lost causes, pointless activities. At most, they are partial enactments, shabbily simulating a past that was itself always a sleight of hand.

The systemic inequity of the international art world could no longer be glossed by universals such as art, Modernism, formalism, quality, ambition, achievement, career, etc. Just because the center was losing its grip, and the peripheries were rebelling, "provincialism" became a telling explanation of the structural unfairness of the system, of the ways the dice were always loaded against the artistic colonies, of how artists both at and outside the center were locked into hierarchies of competition and misinformation while the power to change, or even persist, lay elsewhere.[17] Art & Language publications debated the issue

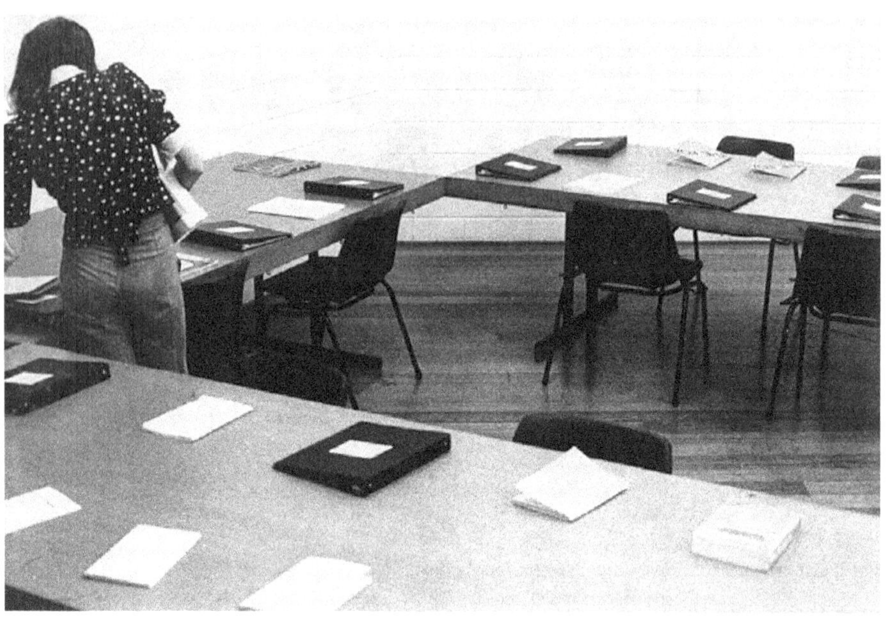

Art & Language, Art & Language, *National Art School, Melbourne, 1975, reading space. Photo: Suzanne Davies.*

of how to best analyze this system in order to develop equitable alternatives, fairer ways of going on as artists—viz. the first and second issues of *The Fox* (New York, 1975).

Other artists were forming groups with similar goals: in New York, for example, artists' groups, along with many individuals, came together for discussions about feasible political effectivity in a loose umbrella coalition called Artists Meeting for Cultural Change. A frequent target was the galleries, public and private, for their museumization of avant-gardism, their commodifying of inventiveness. When *Some Recent American Art*, a survey of mainly minimal art, toured Australia in 1974, it attracted criticism, particularly in Adelaide, as both incomprehensible and culturally imperialist. When Lucy Lippard accompanied the show on its New Zealand tour, she raised these issues herself.[18]

In such a context, when Art & Language was invited to exhibit in the major state galleries in Australia in 1975, the key issue was obvious. The format had to provide an alternative model of an "international art show." It was prefigured in *Soft-Tape* (1966). A politicized concept of translation, acutely alert to cultural difference, took center stage:

> We wanted it to be open, translatable, to establish a learning situation around it—so, above all, we needed a structure which would allow the participants to feed in their reflections on what they are engaged in. As well, though every issue would inevitably come up in an art context, we needed a form which would be loaded towards breaking the limitations and question-begging of that context. Finally, we wanted to examine the technical problems involved in the "cultural noise" which transmitted messages pick up, to see how "translation" functions in such situations.

So the format became the simple one of Ian Burn, Mel Ramsden, and other members of Art & Language New York sending each day for a week telexes of work in progress to a discussion room set up in the exhibiting spaces of the gallery, where I and an invited guest would attempt to embed the text in dialogue with each other and the audience. The 1975 account currently being cited went on to the key issue:

> The core problem is the compartmentalization of our culture(s). A focus for this is the provincialist dependence on metropolitan art models, of which stylistic influences are only the most obvious symptoms. We hoped that by exaggerating the mechanism of sending current New York art information, by sending telexes of work being done at the time by Art & Language New York, the issue would come up in unavoidable ways. And by my presence as "translator" the implications of the exchange would be rendered available for discussion and change in dialogue with me.[19]

The issue of metropolitan power and provincial dependence certainly came up, and with a vengeance. As it happened, the timing of the Sydney and Melbourne shows coincided with the tour of the International Council of the Museum of Modern Art's blockbuster exhibition *Modern Masters: From Manet to Matisse.* N.S.W. Liberal politician Peter Coleman objected, and Art Gallery of N.S.W. trustees and director Peter Laverty cancelled the Art & Language show. In Melbourne, visiting MOMA cu-

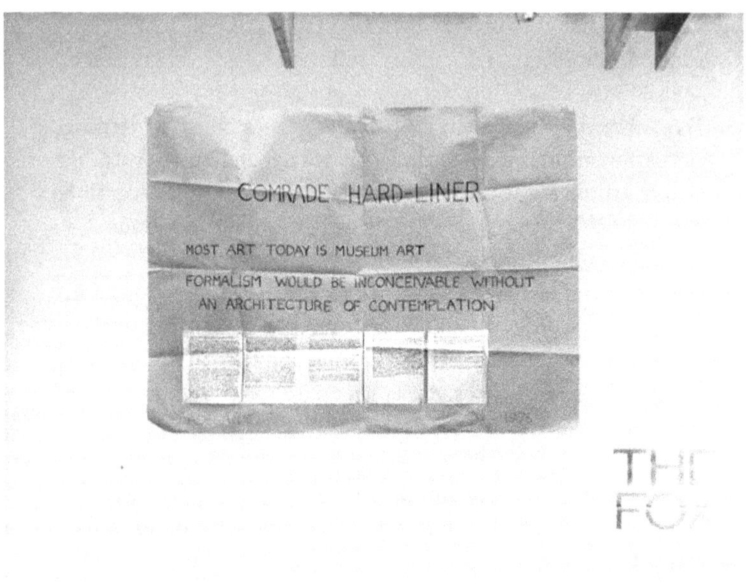

Art & Language, Art & Language, *Art Gallery of South Australia, Adelaide, 1975, installation (Comrade Hard-Liner banner).*

rator William Lieberman threatened to sue the National Gallery of Victoria on the basis of the following paragraph in the poster:

> This latest form of art imperialism can only be assailed by first assailing our given producer-consumer "natures." Are we in good hands with the Museum of Modern Art and the U.S. Information Service, the professionals the specialists the artocrats/bureaucrats who hand us culture, not as something *we* do but as something *they* do, who "creatively" wrap themselves around the creations of others, not something we do but something *they* do?

NGV director Gordon Thompson also caved in but was persuaded by staff to allow its staging in the Art School in back of the Gallery. At the Art Gallery of South Australia the exhibition went ahead as planned: Adelaide was not part of the schedule of *Modern Masters*. These acts of

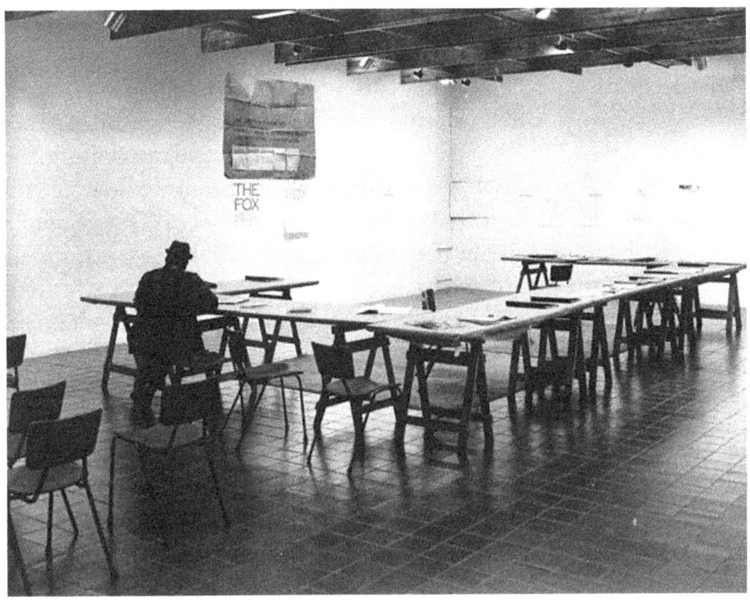

Art & Language (P), Art & Language, *Auckland City Art Gallery, Auckland, 1976, reading space.*

censorship reflect the acute sensitivity of the Modernist masters to the extreme fragility of their culture.

What shapes did translation take in the 1975 Art & Language discussions? The difficulty of Art & Language discourse was often remarked. For some, this signaled pretension, for others, confusion: it was, then, either not worth the effort of translation, or untranslatable. Yet is not the drive to the unrepresentable an absolutely essential avant-garde impulse? Art & Language, like many others at the time, searched for meaning beyond the easy meanings of closed knowledges: was not its commitment to systematically rendering its sociolect incomprehensible to even its own speakers an important strategy to this end? Similarly, the aggressive, even abusive, attacks on everybody else's "bad language" could be seen as an instance of the totalizing negativity essential to any avant-garde breakthrough.

But the first impulse blocked access, and the second bred resentment, both effects being contrary to ease of translation. Furthermore, while one sacrificed translatability in favor of insisting on the significance of the untranslatable, the other presumed a degree of translatability—indeed, of common, if essentially contested, ground—otherwise the attacks would seem mere hysterical shouting, inchoate mouthings. This contradiction is indicative of Art & Language's enforced march from "intersubjectivity" to "praxis," from its internal obsessions to dealing with the wider world, during these years. Similar paths were taken by many artists at the time: it has been convincingly argued that it was Conceptual Art's "failure" to achieve its more abstract goals that led to its more fundamental "success," that its devastating critique of high Modernism laid the groundwork for the much more socially and politically engaged art that followed.[20]

While a significant element in shaping the 1975 shows was to try to embody some of the contradictions and inequalities of the metropolitan/provincial situation, the aim was less to transmit what was going on in New York, more to provoke local self-knowledge. Thus the poster, after describing my role as being to "deal with each blurt praxiologically—concerning himself with the question of embeddedness, the problems of re-embedding, the specific contexts of reference," went on to place the obligation to translate firmly in the hands of the discussants. No longer spectators, nor even audience; everybody was a participant, actively translating willy-nilly.

I set out to be a participant in the pandemonium, not a spokesperson for Art & Language in exile, nor a visitor speaking in transit. I opened the first NGV discussion by saying that I found the telex as problematic as the *Modern Masters* exhibition upstairs. I began the second session by claiming that "one of my roles here is to act as a kind of translator in relation to the blurts sent from NY," then I identified that day's telex as originating from English Art & Language (a surprise to me). This was already an act of translation, which I followed up by a detailed exposition of the key arguments and phrases in the eight-hundred-word transmission. Two quite opposite conceptions of the translator's role are manifest. In the latter case, I was the translator as interpreter, an as-neutral-as-possible mediator. In the former (and, in fact, throughout the actual discussions) I sought a critical independence within the process, constantly changing tack in order to keep the dialogue open. In this way I attempted to challenge a further contradiction implicit in the situation, one endemic to provincialist dependence: the expectation that, after three years in New York I would be transmitting the latest ideas, values, trends, and gossip, whereas my essential message was that the latest from overseas doesn't matter anymore, and that we had to construct our own artistic cultures, here and now, with the fragments available.[21]

Did this amount to a new role for the artist, that of translator, seeking new transformations in the shifting spaces between cultures, spaces shaped by enormous inequities, passionate resistances, subtle compromises, elusive promises? To a degree, yes, but in a more important sense, no. The ambiguities, elisions, and naivetes of trying to act as a wide-open middleman are evident through the texts of the 1975 discussions—as are, I hope, some of its rebarbative, and useful, edges. But more significant was the drive toward the obliteration of the artist as privileged generator of meaning: as translator in this open, reflexive, engaged sense I was less an author of the work in progress, more an agent in the practice of its production. But so, crucially, were the participants: all were enabled, even obliged, to become translators of the discourse as it was happening.

AUCKLAND 1976: "THE WAY YOU WANT IT"

Much changed between May and July 1975, the dates of the Art & Language shows in Australia, and August 1976, when the (Provisional) Art & Language discussion/displays were held in Auckland. Working relations within and between the New York and English groups had soured to such an extent that agreement as to who used the group name when was hotly contested: thus the "(Provisional)" before any work by (certain) members of the New York group, even when showing essentially independently, as I was in Auckland. Of much greater significance was the extraordinarily intense political situation: its impact was felt in all spheres of life and throughout the art world.[22] After the dismissal of the Whitlam Government in November 1975, theoretical modes of working, however semiotically radical, even terroristic, suddenly seemed impossibly esoteric. With many others, I sought much more public spheres—particularly, the mass media—and new, non–art world audiences—in the case of Art & Language in Australia, the labor movement.

I knew (I thought) more about New Zealand politics than I did about New Zealand art. I could call to mind Colin McCahon's and Ralph Hotere's word imagery; it had always seemed to me that the Annandale Imitation Realists' peculiar mixture of wild words and "primitive" imagery was not unconnected with the fact that two of that group's three members—Ross Crothall and Colin Lanceley—were New Zealanders;

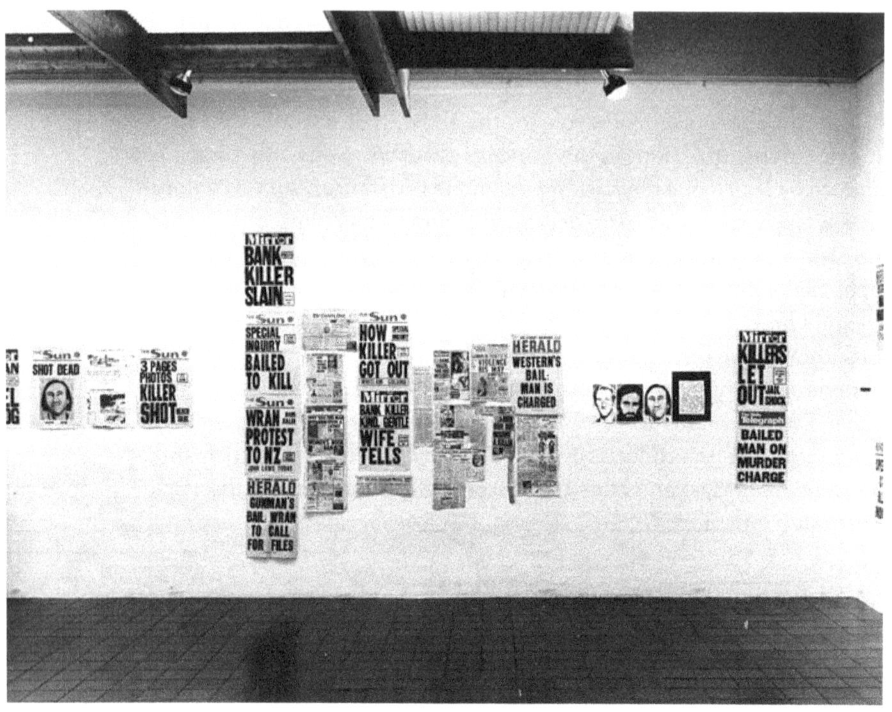

Art & Language (P), Media Massacre, *Art & Language, Auckland City Art Gallery, Auckland, 1976 (detail).*

Billy Apple did occasional nomination pieces about art and money; I had heard that Jim Allen and Bruce Barber built performances around visual/verbal plays; I discovered Nicholas Spill's wild punning. The National Party, having won the 1975 election by a landslide, promptly imposed a wage/price freeze, imposed heavy anti-union legislation, unleashed police squads to send Islanders home, staged a Russian warship scare, and endorsed an All Black tour of South Africa during the Olympic Games. Prime Minister Muldoon governed by contempt, fear, and bluff. "New Zealand—The Way You Want It." There seemed to be sufficient parallels to the new regime in Australia for me to hope that the format of the 1975 shows would work somehow similarly across the Tasman.

There were, however, some major differences. I introduced these in an attempt to obviate—again by the device of exaggeration—the cul-

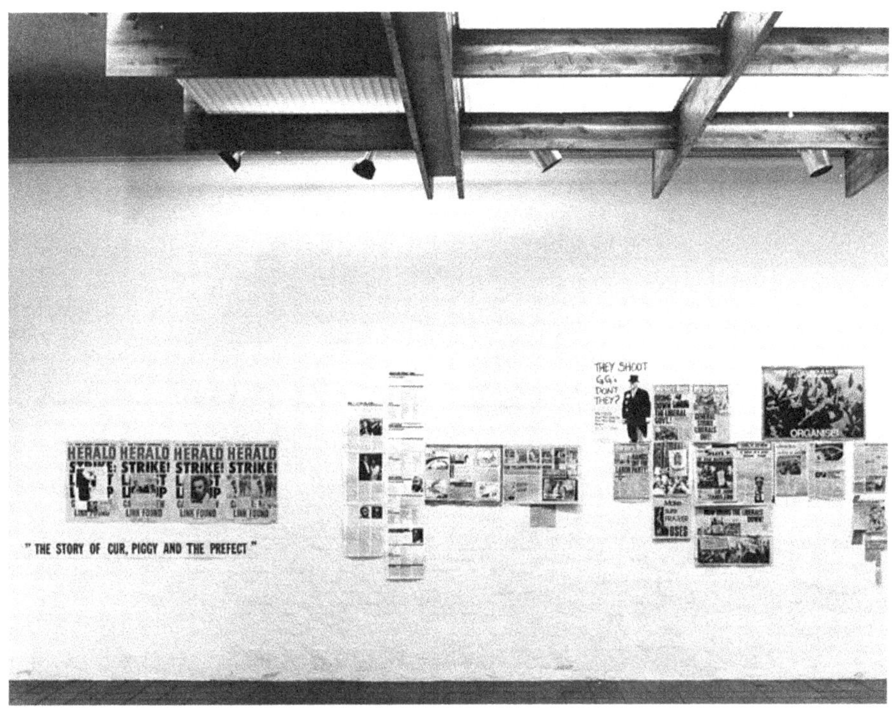

Art & Language (P), The Story of Cur, Piggy and The Prefect, Art & Language, *Auckland City Art Gallery, Auckland, 1976 (detail).*

tural dependence that, I assumed, followed from Australia's economic dominance of the region. As a setting for the discussions, I installed three displays of newspaper posters, one along each wall of the Gallery. *Medibunk* set out the Sydney newspapers' divisive presentation of the general strike against the dismemberment of the national health care system, Medibank, by the Liberal Country Party. *Media Massacre* began with the idea of showing how dimly New Zealand appeared in the Australian press but blew out into a display of the sensationalization of murderer and escapee Phillip Western. *The Story of Cur, Piggy and The Prefect* traced Kerr's coup, Fraser's ascendency, and parallels with Muldoon's reign. Each of these, but particularly the latter, was conceived as a *ta tze pao*, a wall newspaper on the model of the Democracy Wall in China, to which anyone could add their views. Some did.

But before the show could get under way, a censorship farce had to be

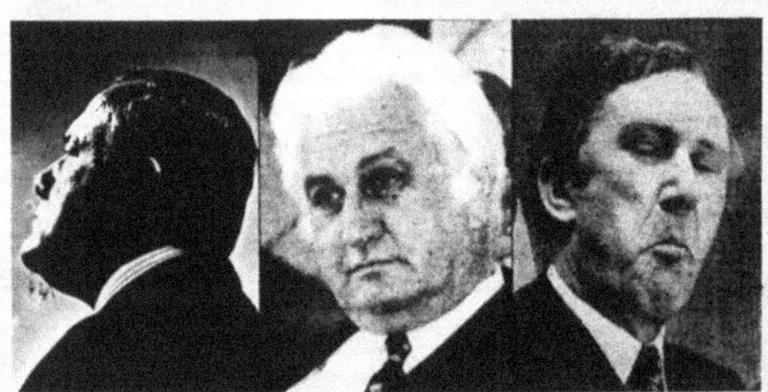

Art & Language (P), Art & Language, *Auckland City Art Gallery, Auckland, 1976, poster (censored). Photographer: Sam Hartnett, courtesy of* ARTSPACE, *New Zealand.*

played out. The poster's centerpiece consisted of three words—"piggy," "cur," and "prefect"—above photographs of Prime Minister Muldoon (taken in the makeup room of a television studio, chosen for its evocation of official portraits of Mussolini), Australian Governor-General Sir John Kerr (taken when drunk at the Melbourne Cup), and Prime Minister Malcolm Fraser (taken when chewing cake during an American Bicentenary Celebration). Disrespectful, critical readings of these men are inevitable when their nicknames are set against such images of them. This proved too much for certain members of the Council and the Gallery committee: the poster and the show itself were banned. After much negotiation, the words in the poster were obliterated, and the show went ahead. My major aim with respect to provoking displays of iron fists within liberal gloves was realized the next day: on the front page of the *Auckland Star* a photograph of the censored poster appeared, alongside a heading that restored the words, and a story about the exhibition being "devoted to rightwing politics in Australia and New Zealand, as well as the impact of the media." Just how ideologically embedded in each other these events were is traced in my piece *Daily Ideology*, commissioned by the National Gallery and shown in *The Word in Art* show, January to March 1978.[23]

Jim and Mary Barr, in their exhibition *When Art Hits the Headlines*, tell only part of the censorship story, and then inaccurately, ending up with an unnecessarily negative conclusion about the powerlessness of political art in galleries.[24] The poster was pasted up around the city before being censored, the blackening out occurred on only a few posters, the posters on display in the Gallery were blackened out, then stamped with a "This has been censored" sign. After the *Auckland Star* story, the tapes blackening out the words were taken off. Sir Dove Meyer Robinson's remark about anything in the Gallery being "in quotation marks" was made in the midst of these events. I was more concerned about him banning the show itself a few days before. At the end of his visit during the installation, he said: "This is an attack on the media, isn't it? I hate the media too. Go right ahead." So, while I agree that the politics that work best in an art gallery are those that deal with the politics of the gallery itself, with the institutions and practices of art, I do not accept the Barrs' conclusion that these are the *only* politics possible. The gallery can be used as a base for more public politics, for the ideological battles, the struggles for the power to signify, which are part of the currency of "real/political life." The Mayor recognized this, both in his comment to

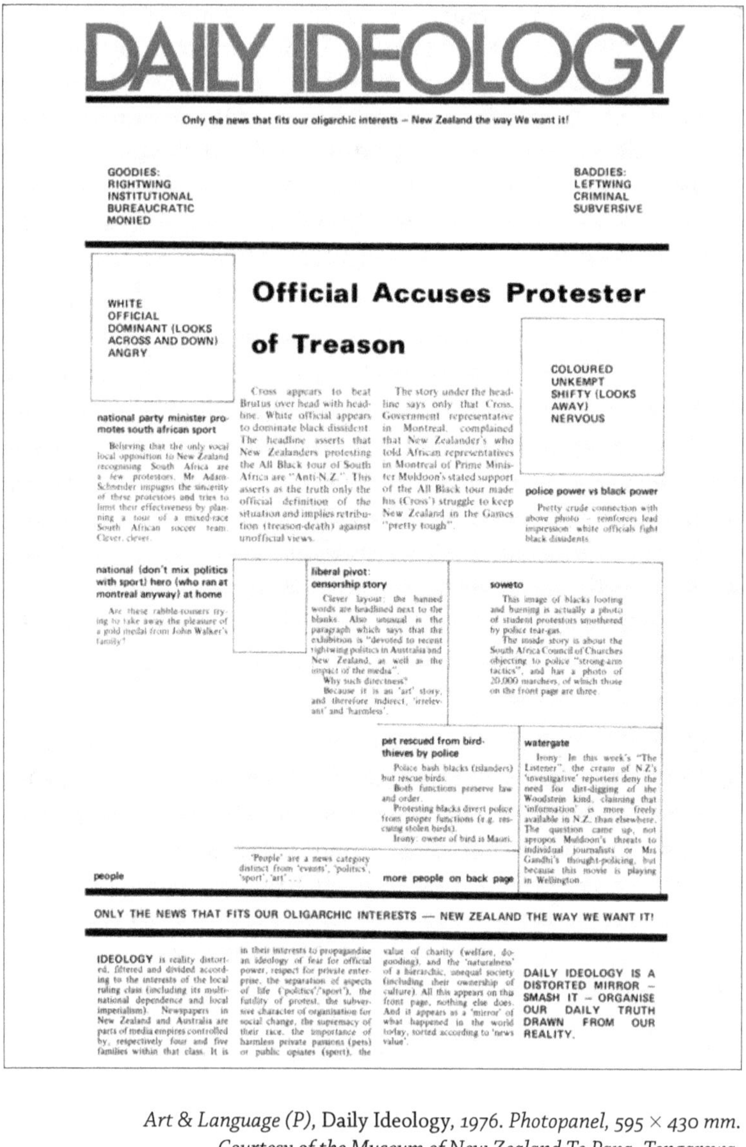

DAILY IDEOLOGY

Only the news that fits our oligarchic interests – New Zealand the way We want it!

GOODIES:
RIGHTWING
INSTITUTIONAL
BUREAUCRATIC
MONIED

BADDIES:
LEFTWING
CRIMINAL
SUBVERSIVE

WHITE
OFFICIAL
DOMINANT (LOOKS ACROSS AND DOWN)
ANGRY

Official Accuses Protester of Treason

COLOURED
UNKEMPT
SHIFTY (LOOKS AWAY)
NERVOUS

Cross appears to beat Brutus over head with headline. White official appears to dominate black dissident. The headline asserts that New Zealanders protesting the All Black tour of South Africa are "Anti-N.Z.". This asserts as the truth only the official definition of the situation and implies retribution (treason-death) against unofficial views.

The story under the headline says only that Cross, Government representative in Montreal, complained that New Zealander's who told African representatives in Montreal of Prime Minister Muldoon's stated support of the All Black tour made his (Cross') struggle to keep New Zealand in the Games "pretty tough".

national party minister promotes south african sport

Believing that the only vocal local opposition to New Zealand recognising South Africa are a few protestors, Mr Adam-Schneider impugns the sincerity of these protestors and tries to limit their effectiveness by planning a tour of a mixed-race South African soccer team. Clever, clever.

police power vs black power

Pretty crude connection with above photo – reinforces lead impression: white officials fight black dissidents.

national (don't mix politics with sport) hero (who ran at montreal anyway) at home

Are these rabble-rousers trying to take away the pleasure of a gold medal from John Walker's family?

liberal pivot: censorship story

Clever layout: the banned words are headlined next to the blanks. Also unusual is the paragraph which says that the exhibition is "devoted to recent rightwing politics in Australia and New Zealand, as well as the impact of the media".

Why such directness?

Because it is an 'art' story, and therefore indirect, 'irrelevant' and 'harmless'.

soweto

This image of blacks looting and burning is actually a photo of student protestors smothered by police tear-gas.

The inside story is about the South Africa Council of Churches objecting to police "strong-arm tactics", and has a photo of 20,000 marchers, of which those on the front page are three.

pet rescued from bird-thieves by police

Police bash blacks (islanders) but rescue birds.

Both functions preserve law and order.

Protesting blacks divert police from proper functions (e.g. rescuing stolen birds).

Irony: owner of bird is Maori.

watergate

Irony: In this week's "The Listener", the cream of N.Z.'s 'investigative' reporters deny the need for dirt-digging of the Woodstein kind, claiming that 'information' is more freely available in N.Z. than elsewhere. The question came up, not apropos Muldoon's threats to individual journalists or Mrs Gandhi's thought-policing, but because this movie is playing in Wellington.

people

'People' are a news category distinct from 'events', 'politics', 'sport', 'art' . . .

more people on back page

ONLY THE NEWS THAT FITS OUR OLIGARCHIC INTERESTS — NEW ZEALAND THE WAY WE WANT IT!

IDEOLOGY is reality distorted, filtered and divided according to the interests of the local ruling class (including its multinational dependence and local imperialism). Newspapers in New Zealand and Australia are parts of media empires controlled by, respectively four and five families within that class. It is in their interests to propagandise an ideology of fear for official power, respect for private enterprise, the separation of aspects of life ('politics'/'sport'), the futility of protest, the subversive character of organisation for social change, the supremacy of their race, the importance of harmless private passions (pets) or public opiates (sport), the value of charity (welfare, do-gooding), and the 'naturalness' of a hierarchic, unequal society (including their ownership of culture). All this appears on this front page, nothing else does. And it appears as a 'mirror' of what happened in the world today, sorted according to 'news value'.

DAILY IDEOLOGY IS A DISTORTED MIRROR – SMASH IT – ORGANISE OUR DAILY TRUTH DRAWN FROM OUR REALITY.

Art & Language (P), Daily Ideology, *1976. Photopanel, 595 × 430 mm. Courtesy of the Museum of New Zealand Te Papa, Tongarewa.*

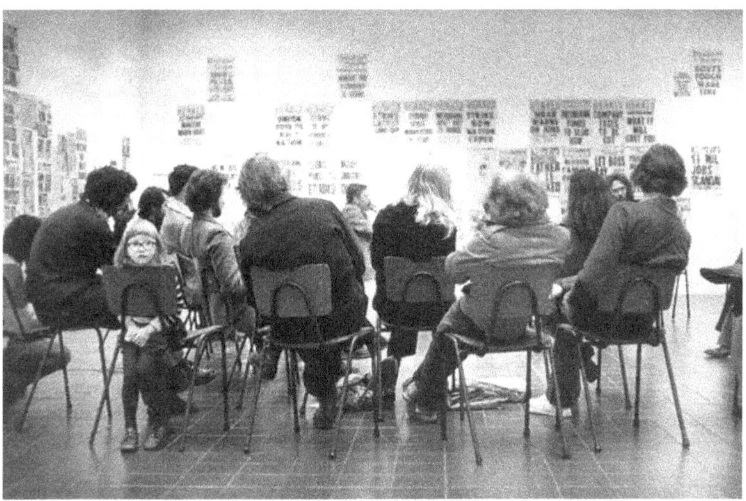

Art & Language (P), Art & Language, *Auckland City Art Gallery, Auckland, 1975, discussion, August 4, 1976.*

me and his quite contrary remark to the press. In politics, people speak with many voices.

The discussions were not structured around blurts from further away, but around the media displays in the gallery space, and the media event of the failed censorship. Art & Language material was available in part of the space as background reading: my distance from it was increasing, so I rarely acted as translator/mediator. The language of the newspaper posters is the ultimate in apparent transparency, so they required little in the way of direct translation, a lot in the way of ideological decoding. This was done by the participants in the discussion—journalists, building workers, artists, critics, academics—in a full-blooded, critical fashion. For a moment, translation was transcended. And this, perhaps, is the best thing that can happen to it.[25]

NOTES

This chapter was originally published as Terry Smith, "The Tasks of Translation: Art & Language in Australia & New Zealand 1975–6," in Ian Wedde and Gregory Burke, eds., Now See Hear! Art, Language and Translation *(Wellington, New Zealand: Victoria University Press, 1990), 250–61.*

1. Walter Benjamin, "The Task of the Translator," in *Illuminations* (New York: Schocken, 1969), 69–82.
2. Walter Benjamin, "The Work of Art in the Age of Mechanical Reproduction," in *Illuminations*, 217–52.
3. Jacques Derrida, "Semiologie et Grammatologie," in *Positions* (Paris: Editions de Minuit, 1972), 31, cited in Gayatri Chakravorty Spivak, "Translator's Preface," in Jacques Derrida, *Of Grammatology* (Baltimore, MD: Johns Hopkins University Press, 1976), lxxxvii.
4. Cited in Alan Bass, "Translator's Introduction," in Jacques Derrida, *Writing and Difference* (London: Routledge and Kegan Paul, 1981), xv.
5. Jacques Derrida, "Plato's Pharmacy," in *Dissemination* (Chicago: University of Chicago Press, 1981).
6. Roland Barthes, "The Death of the Author," in *Image-Music-Text* (London: Fontana, 1977), and Michel Foucault, "What Is an Author?," in *Language, Counter-Memory, Practice* (Ithaca, NY: Cornell University Press, 1977).
7. Lucy R. Lippard, ed., *Six Years: The Dematerialization of the Art Object* (New York: Praeger, 1973).
8. Clement Greenberg's "Modernist Painting" was the key text. It was first published in *Art and Literature* 4 (Spring 1965) and later anthologized in Gregory Battcock, ed., *The New Art* (New York: Dutton, 1966), 66–77.
9. Kosuth's essay first appeared serialized in *Studio International* magazine in October, November, and December 1969. It was later reprinted in Gregory Battcock, ed., *Idea Art* (New York: Dutton, 1973), 70–101.
10. Richard Wollheim, *Art and Its Objects* (Harmondsworth, UK: Pelican, 1970).
11. Terry Smith, "Art and Art and Language," *Artforum* (February 1974): 50.
12. Nelson Goodman, "Review of *Art and Illusion*," *Journal of Philosophy* 57 (1960): 599.
13. Art & Language, *Blurting in A&L* (New York and Halifax: Art & Language Press and Nova Scotia College of Art, 1973), 81–84.
14. Michael Baldwin and Phillip Pilkington, "Handbook(s) for Going-On," *Art-Language* 2, no. 4 (June 1974); and Ian Burn, Mel Ramsden, and Terry Smith, "Draft for an Anti-Textbook," *Art-Language* 3, no. 1 (September 1974).
15. Handbill for *Art & Language* exhibition, National Gallery of Victoria,

Melbourne, May–June 1975, cited in Terry Smith, ed., *Art & Language: Australia 1975* (Sydney: Art & Language Press, 1976), 19.

16. A theme in "Draft for an Anti-Textbook."

17. See my "The Provincialism Problem," *Artforum* (September 1974): 54–59. Subsequent discussions include those about regionalist tendencies in Australian art within and beyond the East Coast capitals, pursued in the magazine *Periphery* edited by Geoff Levitus, and the debate between myself and Bernice Murphy following the 1988 Sydney Biennale, published in the August, October, and December 1988 issues of *Art Monthly*.

18. Lucy Lippard, "Notes on Seeing Some Recent American Art in New Zealand," *Auckland City Art Gallery Quarterly* 59 (1975): 2–3.

19. Terry Smith, "Fighting Modern Masters," *The Fox* 2 (1975): 15–21; also in Smith, *Art & Language: Australia 1975*, 1–4.

20. Ian Burn, "The 'Sixties: Crisis and Aftermath," *Art & Text* 1 (Autumn 1981): 49–65.

21. Detailed transcripts of the discussions are in Smith, *Art & Language: Australia 1975*. A display of this last point is my "Art Criticism/Self Criticism," in *6th Mildura Sculpture Exhibition* (Mildura, Australia: Mildura Art Centre, 1975), 1–10.

22. See my "Art Criticism in Australia: The Mid-1970s Moment," in Robyn McKenzie, ed., *Art Papers: The Present and Recent Past of Australian Art and Criticism*, supplement to *Agenda* 2 (August 1988): 12–13.

23. For a contemporary reaction to the show, see Geoff Chapple, *The Independent* (November 6, 1976). My account of these events, plus extracts from the discussions, appears in Charles Merewether and Ann Stephen, eds., *The Great Divide* (Melbourne: Great Divide, 1977), 48–53, and *Left Curve* 7 (1978): 66–72. I would like to pay tribute to John Maynard's crucial role throughout, and to Bruce and Pauline Barber for their support.

24. Jim and Mary Barr, *When Art Hits the Headlines* (Wellington, New Zealand: National Art Gallery, 1987), 13.

25. Translation came up subsequently as a term more accurate than "appropriation" in describing recent post-postmodern art strategies: see "The Life-Motif, Interview with Imants Tillers," in *Imants Tillers: Works 1978–1988* (London: Institute of Contemporary Art, 1988). But Tillers still ties it to the old mythologies of the artist as privileged creator, as key author of the discourse, however much it consists of the already-said. On more pertinent thinking about translation, especially in "post-cultural" situations, where more subtle analyses than those of metropolitan/provincial, center/periphery cultural imperialism are necessary, see *Meanjin* 4 (1989), especially Simon During's essay "What Was the West?" (also published in a longer version in *Sport* 4 [Autumn 1990]), which includes interesting analyses of the complexities of communications between New Zealand cultural groups.

A Conversation about Conceptual Art, Subjectivity, and the *Post-Partum Document* 3

TERRY SMITH: There are very few artists still practicing now whose work, however transformed, remains shaped—in its basic parameters, perhaps—by that moment in the early 1970s when it seemed possible to achieve what we then called "praxis": to fuse theory and practice, to evolve a theoretical practice as art, to do art-theoretical work. I recall that David Antin once picked out the most enterprising work of the 1960s as *performative*—I think he had in mind happenings, performance work, maybe even his and Ian Wilson's speech pieces—or *processual*—which meant actions or environments displaying natural systems, such as Hans Haacke's early work—or *procedural*—all those nominations of a series of actions, or sequence of thoughts, logical strings, ranging from scripts for performances to Richard Long's walks, or Huebler's social measurement mappings. Another term, *propositional* practices, needs to be added to pick up the essential character of language-based conceptualism. This was emphasized by Joseph Kosuth in the second issue of *Art-Language*, when he tried to distinguish the work which he and the English originators of Art & Language were doing from artists in what they called the Seth Siegelaub stable (Andre, Weiner, Barry, Huebler, et al.).

These four terms are useful pointers to the forms of practice then, but I believe that content was—as always—crucial. Right from the mid-1960s, the driving template, if you like, was to work on the concept of art, to test the possibilities for art practices which would be metadiscursive, and to use languages of various kinds to that end. So Art & Language–

type work, for example, was initially an *analytic* practice, developing propositions about the possibilities for art practice, first through interrogating imagined or actualized theoretical objects, then through examining imagined theories and theories of imagining, or, better, of theorizing. In the early 1970s, however, things shifted. Analytical work continued, but it became also *synthetic* in the sense that the practice was expanded to become an inquiry into subjects and experiences which were much broader than art and its languages, and, of course, into theories for thinking, for speaking, these subjects and experiences. This is an obvious impact of the social movements of the 1960s.

Examples of this shift would be Hans Haacke, obviously. Less obvious, but important, is the trajectory of Art & Language work itself, especially in New York and then Australia from 1975–76. But it happens all over the world, in Central Europe, in Latin America, for example, sometimes earlier, sometimes later. The conceptual-political connection occurs as a split, or a displacement, or as a nexus, depending on the local context. I see your *Post-Partum Document* very much in this context.

MARY KELLY: When I started work on *Post-Partum Document* in 1973 I was curious about the parallels with Art & Language work in England. They were very influential, as was the work of Kosuth in New York. I did want to shift the emphasis from the notion of the analytical proposition to a more synthetic process. This is a much more complex argument than simply saying that I was going to reintroduce life into art. Your own terms for understanding Conceptual Art—where you set up the idea of a practice concerned with interrogating the conditions of existence for its own interrogation—make a lot of sense to me. In my case, obviously, the founding condition is an investigation of the subject. This was coincident with the kinds of questions being asked outside of art, by Marxism and feminism. The very first piece that I did, called *Introduction to the Post-Partum Document*, used found objects. Previous conceptual work had remained rather distant from that kind of materiality.

That was one of the first big departures from the established conceptual esthetic. Another was the decision to not use photography. I wanted to emphasize what was affectively, emotionally loaded about this relation that I was documenting. But, then, when I superimposed the Lacanian schema over the baby vests, I don't think that, at the very first moment, I knew exactly how controversial—or even consequential—this juxtaposition would be. It began as a very insistent and almost intuitive attempt to bring the desire—you could say—for theory (itself very, very embryonic as far as its use in the women's movement was concerned at that time) together with the cathexis of the everyday experience of mothering. *Post-Partum Document* was the first work that I know of to introduce Lacanian references so explicitly, but there isn't a significant division here between the emotional effect of theory and the emotional effect of objects, between the ability of material objects to be fabricated or organized theoretically and for a theory to have its materiality. There's a certain breaking down of these discrete domains by bringing them together.

T.S.: Putting it that way makes me want to set out a little more fully how I see the unfoldings of Conceptual Art. Not exactly in phases, or cut-and-dried periods, but the first significant moves of conceptualism, occurred, I believe, between 1965 and 1969 and were—it is often forgotten—object-directed. Paradoxically, of course—or, better, through a doubling. You remember that a lot of people, then, were working at the edges of minimalism or performance or anti-form sculpture or environmental art or earthworks, in ways supplementary to the work that we saw as achieving style under those headings, inspired by it but wanting to maintain a distance from the specifics of the incorporating processes operating in each case. Well, one move was to create impossible objects, things that might, for example, embody the morphological characteristics of any artwork but only those, or consist of the general characteristics of every artwork but none of the specifics. Some of these, like Nauman's, were emotional objects, with somatic psychic residue. But most were theoretical objects, instantiating speculation about art itself. Like algebraic solids, or DNA models. This is where language became so crucial. Early Art & Language work—the impossible objects made, or conceived, by those who first formed Art & Language in Coventry and elsewhere in England, and those in Melbourne, New York, and elsewhere who joined the group or did related work—was about examining the conditions for producing just those kinds of objects. The next move—although some had already made it before 1969—was to interrogate the conditions for the interrogation of what it was to produce those kinds of objects. This doubled meta-discursivity is, to me, the key to language-based, or analytic, conceptualism.

M.K.: But how did this relate to the social, psychoanalytic, and experiential emphases I was suggesting?

T.S.: It was as if a commitment to pure experimentality, to radical interrogation of everything in its most specific forms, was enough. . . . We assumed that the articulation between these would take care of itself, would just, somehow, happen. It took many of us until the early 1970s to realize how wrong we were. This was partly an impact of feminism, partly because the crisis of capitalism then was even deeper than we had thought.

M.K.: For me, the impossible objects you talk about were still unitary rather than relational. For instance, in the *Document*, the intersubjective object was the speech of the child. The pre-condition for that investigation—that is, of language—is already put in place, but not as a question of how we come to be speaking subjects, and how that becoming positions us as men or women.

T.S.: You're right, subjectivity in this sense was largely lacking from the first two moments of Conceptual Art . . .

M.K.: The significance of the relation between the psychic and the social was made obvious to me by its absence in Art & Language work in England, in Kosuth's work. . . . I saw that space as being open.

T.S.: It became increasingly obvious to some of us in Art & Language as well, although there was a huge reluctance to embrace psychoanalysis. There was an assumption, shared by most of us engaged in public sphere politics, including the varieties of Marxism, even anarchism, that whatever happened in that sphere would override the private, or should. There was perhaps also a masculinist suspicion of what seemed an invitation to confusion in "the personal is the political." A fear of loss of power, not unfounded. On the other hand, Freudian psychoanalysis, institutionalized or not, did not seem self-evidently the royal road to a political solution. Instead, we became deeply concerned with indexical processes, with understanding what was at stake in regarding ourselves as a language-embedded, language-producing community. We set the measurement routines of formal language-logics, and the analyses of ordinary language, against the actual chaos of our own conversations.

M.K.: The linguistic theories that seem to predominate initially in the art world were positivistic. But there was already, in France, the development of semiotics. I was part of that trajectory because of my associations with people in film as well as other women in the movement who were interested in the relations between semiotic linguistics and psychoanalysis. I remember when I published the first writing about the *Document* in *Control Magazine* in 1977. Steve Willett's magazine was a perfect example of this information theory attitude towards language, yet it was flexible enough to include my writing. Semiotics is, perhaps, the tendency that predominates now—or, at least it did, through the 1980s. But in the period that we're talking about it was just being introduced in a way that was rather confrontational. Even within the women's movement psychoanalytic theory was not at all accepted. In the early 1970s it started to come out, when Ros Coward and Juliet Mitchell and others insisted on its uses for feminism—it was very hotly debated. So, the key contexts of the *Document* were the relations it had to linguistic theories in the art world and to the questions of socialization raised in the women's movement. In both cases, there was an insistence on certain shifts, most specifically focused on that impossible object, which Freud called the unconscious, and the body of theory appropriate to it, that is, psychoanalysis.

I wanted to go back to the discussion of Art & Language and ask how far you think they went with what you call the synthetic proposition?

T.S.: Well, I suppose it began in the early 1970s with the move into indexing in England, and the Annotations and Blurting projects in New York. The shift is that the work became conversations not only about the concept of art, and about the conditions for interrogating it, but about the art world, about political change and its impact on our practice. To some degree they were about language and subjectivity, about the formation of speakers, about what we called the *idiolect*—pursuing the implications of the idea that each person had their own particular way of speaking—but you could also say this as *ideolect* and thus pick up subjectivization, or interpellation, through ideology: the subject spoken by the state, of and by official language-use. Not by the "beginnings" of speech, as Lacan has it. By 1974 Ian Burn, Mel Ramsden, and I were writing an issue of *Art-Language* which began from social speech but became a conversation about international politics, provincialism, individualism, the modernist art machine, etc. Certainly in New York these were the great points of debate—as is obvious in such formations as the Artists Meeting for Cultural Change. But these happened late in New York, artists' unions had sprung up, as you know from your experience in London, all over the place.

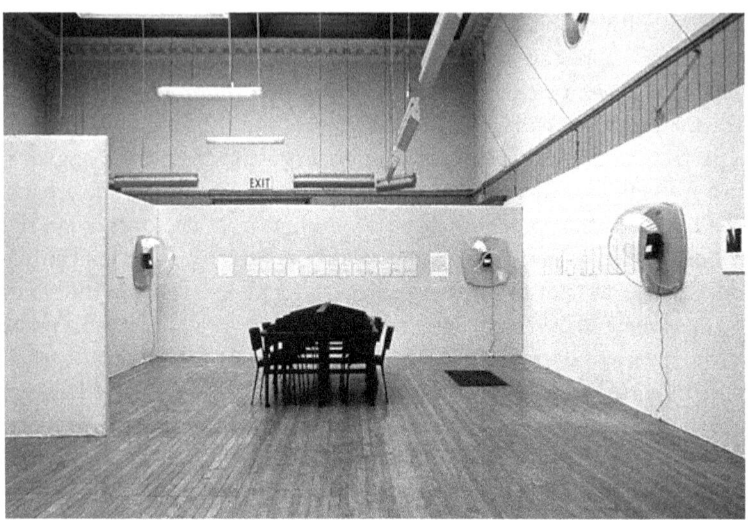

Kay Fido, Margaret Harrison, and Mary Kelly, Women and Work, a Document on the Division of Labor in Industry, 1973–75. *Installation view, South London Art Gallery. Photo: Ray Barrie.*

As to the form of such work, it became less propositional, and, indeed, less procedural. The time for issuing instructions for "actions" other people might take was well past. Frankly, it became very difficult to produce public work—that is, find forms of display—that seemed adequate to the social work of the conversations. Yet the desire to do so was crucial: the turn, or re-turn, of conceptual artists to political practice in the mid-1970s is a major move, one which has driven much of the significant art done since. For me, your earlier project *Women and Work* and the *Post-Partum Document* come out of a similar moment in England.

M.K.: *Women and Work* was an installation which documented the divisions of labor in the metal box industry during the implementation of Equal Pay legislation. For me, it was clearly related to Haacke's *Shapolsky Real Estate* project. But neither it nor *Post-Partum Document* is usually seen as a conceptual work, is it? Rather, as the product of a certain moment in feminist art—usually the one after the moment in which it was produced. It was made in the 1970s, yet is normally seen as representing the shift in feminist art into more theoretical concerns around 1980.

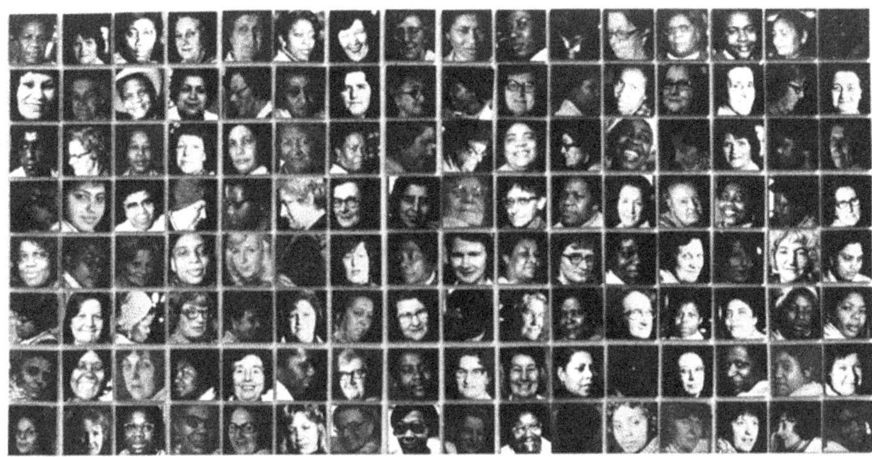

Kay Fido, Margaret Harrison, and Mary Kelly, Women and Work, a Document on the Division of Labor in Industry, *1973–75. Portraits of women metal-box workers, 134 black and white photographs, each 8 × 8 inches.*

Sometimes it seems that the particular moment of a work's reception—in the United States—is more definitive than the moment of its creation. In this case, it eclipses even the scandal of *Post-Partum*'s first reception: the "Bricks and nappies" controversy when it was shown at the Institute of Contemporary Art in London in 1976.

T.S.: Cultural imperialism rides again! I see *Post-Partum Document* as primarily conceptual work, definitely in its form: it's organized to track various activities, that is, procedurally. Its organizational logic is presumed to be larger than the subject or the person doing the tracing. It's processual in that its subject—motherhood—is itself normally figured as a natural process. Yet the procedures you follow, or set out, seem to cut against any sense of natural flow, seem placed against the instinctual. There is a kind of manic restraint, a withholding, an initial distancing which nevertheless hopes to surprise some otherwise inaccessible information or attitudes along the way. This mood is typical of procedural work from the late '60s onwards.

Some people probably did read the *Document* as about natural forces, and were shocked by its cognitive armature. To me, it's a work of the-

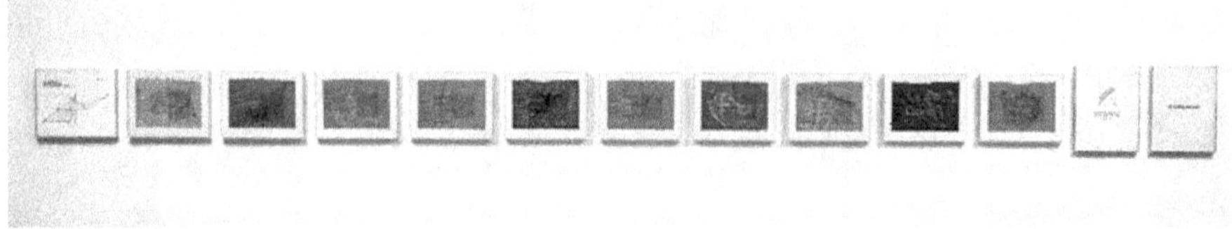

Mary Kelly, Post-Partum Document. Analysed Markings and Diary Perspective Schema (Experimentum Mentis III: Weaning from the Dyad), *1975. Collage, pencil, crayon, chalk, and printed diagrams on paper. Displayed: 36 × 583 cm. Tate Gallery. Photo Credit: Tate, London/Art Resource, NY.*

ory, in the sense that it shows theory at work in your daily life, actively constructing the sort of relations involved in having children, being a mother. Mothering is a theoretically informed practice in an absolutely saturated way. Dr. Spock, or Penelope Leach, anyone?

Another Conceptual-Art aspect of the *Document* is that it enables—in fact, obliges—the spectator to experience theory, to relate to what's happening via theory as the only way of grasping what's going on.

M.K.: Right, the *Document* follows, in your terms, typical procedural forms, tracing events such as feeding every hour, every day, or taping the linguistic exchanges between mother and child. This might look developmental, but what I always call the pseudo-scientific discourse is countered by the reference to the Lacanian diagram. In the Footnotes "Experimentum Mentis" sections I introduced a different theorization of that moment, which was much more connected to the debate around psychoanalysis and feminism. The Art & Language indexes, although they might have touched on questions that moved outside of esthetics, still seemed to me to remain within the discourse of the fine art institutions. The installation of the *Document* was intended to be polemical with the Art & Language *Index*. My idea was that you would go to the Footnotes for information, but rather than a system of internal referencing, it would raise issues which related to the social movements of the time.

T.S.: That's important, but a response might be that if you look closely at the *Index*, or many other conceptual works right from the mid-1960s, you will find that systemization always has one or two random terms

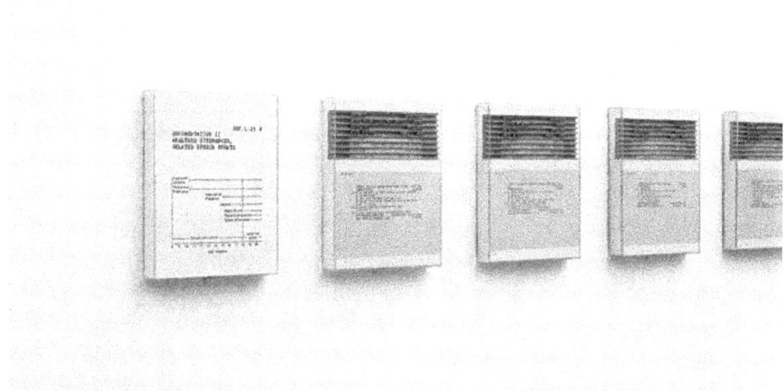

Exhibition view, Mary Kelly. Post-Partum Document. The Complete Work (1973–79), *Generali Foundation, Vienna, 1998, showing part of* Documentation II: Analysed Utterances and Related Speech Events, *1975. © Generali Foundation Collection. Photo: Werner Kaligofsky.*

in it, or that its structural regularity is aimed at provoking, even generating, some kind of dyssystemic irrationality. The craziness of things in the world. The randomness of structures. The irreality of the real. These were what drew us—more and more, especially in the early to mid-1970s. So it's not an obsession with order, but a thirst towards a catacrexic disordering of pictures . . .

M.K.: For some people, the *Document* was a catacrexic disordering of motherhood.

T.S.: Yes, mothering appears in an environment of manic intensity!

M.K.: And once you take the discourse to that extreme it almost turns itself inside out, it's hardly recognizable as coming out of that procedural method.

T.S.: I was also thinking about Adrian Piper's work in the early 1970s. It, too, focused on identity-formation, confronting people on the street, glancing off a connection with them. Somewhat like what she is doing now, but in forms that were more singular, and less to do with racism, from memory.

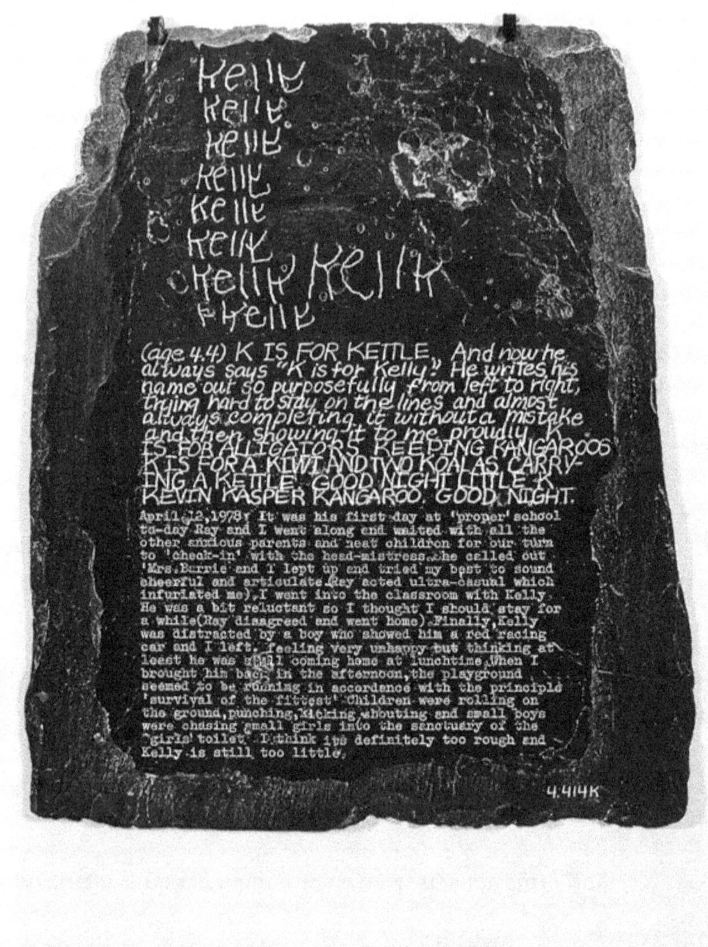

Mary Kelly, Post-Partum Document, *1973–79,* Documentation VI: Pre-Writing Alphabet, Exergue and Diary / Experimentum Mentis VI: (On the Insistence of the Letter), *1978–79 (detail). Arts Council Collection, Southbank Centre, London © the artist.*

M.K.: Aside from her, there were very few artists doing performance work in rigorously theoretical ways. I'm thinking of Gina Pane's *Sentimental Actions*, or Vito Acconci's *Following Piece*, where the question of subjectivity did come into it.

T.S.: Subjectivity was one route that early language-based Conceptual Art didn't take. Nauman was exceptional. By 1969 at least he was casting bits and pieces of body space, setting up those harrowing performance rooms, or observational spaces, where sometimes recorded statements operated as a kind of surveillance-voice. They weren't widely known then, but they were part of the first, analytic move of conceptualism in that they were very much about the spectator in space in relation to an object. The degree of psychic, unconscious, actually traumatic emphasis was unusual for conceptualism. As it was in Acconci.

M.K.: This junction, where performance-oriented work had taken on in some way the question of subjectivity, and conceptual work had developed a kind of theoretical, procedural rigor, is exactly what I wanted to come together in the *Document*. It had the procedural look of Conceptual Art, but fundamentally it engaged with the kinds of issues that predominated in performance work.

T.S.: I want to return to the question of power distributed according to gender in those days. There was an appalling lack of space for women artists in the early "thrust" (I have to say) of conceptualism. This led to some blinkered perceptions, which still echo. Hanne Darboven's work, for example, was seen as a screen of pseudo-language, as something decorative that would never become meaningful. It ended up as a general sign for obsessiveness. Yet in the late 1980s she exhibited a series which interspersed photographs of library spaces with her usual sequences of written pages . . .

M.K.: But her work amounts to much more than just, say, foregrounding obsession. It's the concentrated intensity of the activity which has power. She lets that quality become quite clear as having a level on which, while entirely subjective, is also completely determined by something outside of scientific discourse, although she never states that very explicitly.

T.S.: As if her books were being written by forces outside of her? They do seem runic.

M.K.: The perception of her work has been very male dominated, perhaps.

T.S.: This is a serious issue because in a certain sense she has been figured as someone whose work had the look of Conceptual Art, but none of the content. Another instance of historical gendering?

I wonder how this might come up in relation to the *Post-Partum Document*? One point of view, perhaps masculinist, would presume that its subject—motherhood—is a domain of social experiencing, bodily feeling, emotional diversification, etc., which is both specific to each individual, and also widespread. Not universal, but quite fundamental, basic if anything is, miasmic. So you were faced with the possibility of this project roaming in every direction. Against this chaotic yet bounded prospect you set your methods of regulation, which posit flows, and escaping from regulation. Nothing like a flow escapes from the look of the *Document*, or from its mode of presentation. But flows do erupt in the way many people responded to it, especially to its message about motherhood—which does seem at the heart of what most people take to be natural—being constructed. Many, including me, reacted by reading the work itself as closed: how could motherhood be subject to this cool, withdrawn, unemotional analysis? Maybe our response was one of shocked displacement from the realization that motherhood—even motherhood!—was not a natural but social, psychic, linguistic construction.

M.K.: It is what I was saying earlier about the affective force of the idea, that it should be taken on—as you would say—as part of the interrogation of the conditions of interrogation as such. It's not divided up into some neat masculinity/femininity, theory/practice binary, but is a rather chaotic, anarchic, impositional structure of drives and desires that I continue to be interested in. All of my work has, I think, a certain tension between ordering and losing control.

T.S.: True, but even as far back as Sol LeWitt's first sentences, or Dan Graham's late 1960s poem projects, an anti-analytic relativism was present.

M.K.: If that's the case then the move to subjectivity in the *Document* should have seemed a logical step. For many, it seemed to go too far . . .

T.S.: You must had have people criticizing you for dealing with, and very clearly valuing, motherhood, when lots of women thought of it as a total trap, an anti-feminist way to go. And for doing so in a way that was intensely and obviously theoretical in its mode of address.

M.K.: Well, in one sense that dilemma just put me squarely in the old tradition of the avant-garde transgression. Yet part of the point of conceptualism, you remember, was to change the distribution of interpretative power in the art world, to restore some of it to artists. Certainly to try to influence the ways it would be institutionally received. What amazes me now, looking back, is how little control you do have, finally.

T.S.: The other side of the dilemma for some viewers was the very fact of the subject—motherhood—being made so central in such a sustained way in the *Document* when among the women whom I was closest to at the time, the idea of motherhood—while not necessarily ruled out in practice—was certainly not seen as a likely, or even possible, subject for art. By introducing such material, such a central subjectivity, the *Document* signals a major break with the main concerns of early conceptualism.

NOTE

This chapter was originally published as Terry Smith with Mary Kelly, "A Conversation about Conceptual Art, Subjectivity and the Post-Partum Document," *in Alexander Alberro and Blake Stimson, eds.,* Conceptual Art: A Critical Anthology *(Cambridge, MA: MIT Press, 1999), 450–58. Republished courtesy of The MIT Press.*

REFERENCES

Burn, Ian, Mel Ramsden, and Terry Smith. "Draft for an Anti-Textbook." *Art-Language* 3, no. 1 (September 1974).

Coward, Rosalind, and John Ellis. *Language and Materialism: Developments in Semiology and the Theory of the Subject*. London: Routledge and Kegan Paul, 1977.

Harrison, Charles. *Essays on Art & Language*. Oxford: Blackwell, 1991.
Kelly, Mary. *Footnotes and Bibliography, Post-Partum Document*. London: Institute of Contemporary Art, 1976.
———. "Notes on Reading the *Post-Partum Document*." *Control Magazine* 10 (1977).
———. *Post-Partum Document*. London: Routledge and Kegan Paul, 1983.
Kosuth, Joseph. "Introductory Note by the American Editor." *Art-Language* 1, no. 2 (February 1970).
Mitchell, Juliet. *Psychoanalysis and Feminism*. New York: Pantheon, 1974.
Smith, Terry. "Art and Art and Language." *Artforum* (February 1974): 49–52.

4

Peripheries in Motion

Conceptualism and Conceptual Art in Australia and New Zealand

The presumption that there was a single metropolitan center of invention, out from which artistic innovation spread as a style to be adopted by provincial art worlds, is being tested by this entire exhibition. I believe it will show that, on the contrary, there was a roughly simultaneous emergence in a number of art centers and art communities around the world of a conceptual questioning of the nature of art. In every case, but differently, these seem to have been set against both generalizing notions of art, and modernism perceived as an orthodox, international art discourse. Artists such as Terry Atkinson, Michael Baldwin, and others in Coventry, and Ian Burn and Mel Ramsden in Melbourne, were responding to certain developments in avant-garde art, especially in New York and particularly the anti-form aspect of minimalism. The crucial distinction here may be that they did not reproduce a local version of minimalism but used some of its less mainstream aspects to question art itself.

One of the original conditions of mid-1960s conceptualism is that it was produced in cities such as London and New York by artists such as Ian Burn from Melbourne and Billy Apple from Auckland, that is, by individuals striving to define an art practice distinctive for travelers between the peripheries and centers of cultural power. Much art of this period came out of a suitcase, or could be made on the spot by people in transit. Regions such as the southern Pacific are also important in that they exemplify another worldwide phenomenon: the impact of conceptualism—especially as it became institutionalized as Conceptual Art—on younger artists in local art worlds tied to metropolitan centers. International in form, their work was local in content. This moment still marks out advanced art in the region and, as such, has been subject to commentary by certain Aboriginal artists.

CONTEXT

Since the settlement of Terra Australis and New Zealand by British colonists in the late eighteenth century, the fundamentals and outer boundaries of art practice have been set by commitments to certain subjects (above all landscape), to specific media (especially painting), and to Romantic, self-expressive conceptions of what it is to be an artist. Western European visual forms and institutions dominated national cultural agendas, tying settler and immigrant artists to a framework of provincial dependence on metropolitan centers, especially London. Indigenous visual cultures were posited as exotic others and as generalized emblemata.

All of this began to unravel in the 1960s: popular and high art from the United States assumed cultural leadership, but this prerogative was soon contested at home, in the colonies, and around the world. At the height of its internationalizing reach, U.S. definitions of art—including the institutionalized modernism that was its most advanced form—underwent a crisis of legitimacy. At the same time, following their own imperatives, Aborigines in Australia and Maoris in New Zealand began to assert their cultural singularity, political independence, and historical precedence. Coincidentally, travel by artists back and forth on the colonial circuits, and laterally to other cultural formations, increased markedly, as did the circulation of information about what was happening in art all over the world.[1]

The conceptual "moment" in the art of Australia and New Zealand occurred in the context of these world changes, and was much marked by them. It took, however, quite specific structural forms, three of which I detail here.

1. The idea of the avant-garde emerged, arguably for the first time in the history of Australian and New Zealand art, as the leading model for innovative artmaking. Pop tendencies—themselves relatively weak compared to those in the United States, Britain, and parts of Europe—had produced little in the way of coolly reflexive art. The junk assemblages of the Annandale Imitation Realists celebrated instinctive gatherings of non-art material, especially in the work of Colin Lanceley and Mike Brown. The third member, Ross Crothall, did produce a few works that might count as proto-conceptual. These include his cigarette ab-

stractions, in which actual cigarettes are arrayed in op art formats on hardboard. This group—two New Zealanders and an Australian—came together in 1961–62 for two exhibitions in Melbourne and Sydney, then disbanded after less than a year.[2]

The hard-edge painters and sculptors who gathered around Central Street Gallery in Sydney from 1966—Tony McGillick, Michael Johnson, David Aspden, and others—were an institutionalizing avant-garde in that they subscribed totally to a formalist internationalism. The early conceptualism of Burn and Apple was occurring elsewhere. Whereas the conceptual, process, and performance artists who formed Inhibodress in Sydney in 1970—for instance, Peter Kennedy, Mike Parr, Tim Johnson—were an open, dematerializing avant-garde.[3] All of these developments were driven by a very specific notion of the avant-garde: the belief that, while high-profile recognition, financial success, and cultural power were evidently concentrated in the art capitals of the world, something more important and far-reaching could be achieved by artists at the margins. The nature of art itself could be transformed as a result of the efforts of a group of artists working consciously together, and this could occur in Australia, New Zealand, anywhere. The core impulse of avant-gardism was not, many artists believed, compatible with money and power, particularly not within the nexus of the military-industrial-commercial complex and the culture of high modernism.[4] Art could be rethought in one's head, with the least resources. Look at the Dadaists, at Tatlin's productivists!

The idea that art work could be—indeed, *must* be—conceptual work on the concept of art had profoundly disruptive effects on art practice in Australia and New Zealand during the later 1960s. To make art that itself raises this issue is *to create theoretical objects or events*. This was done, in the mid-1960s, by a very small number of Australian and New Zealand artists in transit.

2. There is no simple shift from object- to idea-based art, anywhere in the world. To define conceptualism in such a way is to descend into banality. On the contrary, the first "step" taken by any art that deserves the name *conceptual* was to make objects—artworks—that threw perception into doubt. In the Australian case, this was expressed at the level of style as an interrogation of minimal painting (including op and hard edge), and of painted metal sculpture (together seen as formalism). This is an originary moment for Conceptual Art as a whole, one of many that happened spontaneously in a number of places around the world during this time. It occurred in 1966 in London, the traditional place for

the continuing education of graduating Australian and New Zealand art students of ambition. Fresh from the National Gallery School in Melbourne, Ian Burn (an Australian) continued his working relationship with the English artist Mel Ramsden, who had just returned from a visit to Australia where he had studied briefly at the same school.

The step to be taken, particularly in the Australian case, was beyond an expanded kind of minimalism, itself the dominant international and local art of the moment among experimental artists. This was not an instant overturning, but a *supplement*, a rendering radically provisional of the host. In New Zealand, there was a greater orientation toward installation and especially performance work in its conceptual currents, reflecting the influential examples of Billy Apple, Jim Allen, Bruce Barber, and others.

3. Conceptualism was one of the defining elements of the shift within the region from a locally focused to internationalist, specifically late modernist, orientation toward art practice. To make art that situates itself in relation to this relationship is to make *strategic objects or events*.

This, too, was done by very few artists during the mid-1960s. But it became a widespread practice throughout the region in the years around 1970. Older artists were deeply disturbed by this trend, yet younger artists flocked to its possibilities in droves. For them, strategic conceptualism was one option among others offered by the proliferation of practices around 1970. Not a choice among new styles—as things must have appeared to younger artists around 1910—but a choice among anti-stylistic actions. Ironically, at the very same moment, conceptualism was being defined into a style: Conceptual Art. The time lags of the international art circuit meant that younger artists based in Australia and New Zealand were confronted with both at once: conceptualism and Conceptual Art. Most chose to try out the new style, but the substantial artists among them saw that conceptualism demanded a new practice.

I will now explore each of these steps in turn.

EARLY CONCEPTUALISM

Barrie Bates received a New Zealand Government Scholarship in 1959 and attended the Royal College of Art in London for the next three years. This school was the site of the invention of British pop, then experiencing a burst of popular and art-world attention.[5] His major focus was graphic art—indeed, advertising was how he made his living—but in 1960 he began to be interested in the idea that everyday activities such as

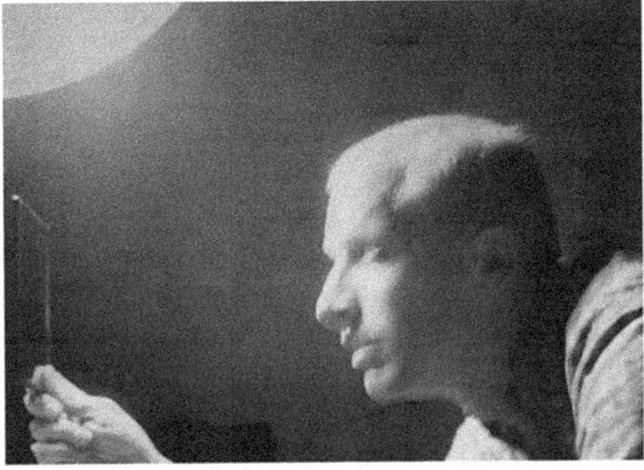

Billy Apple, Bleaching with Lady Clairol Instant Crème Whip, *November 1962. Black and white vintage silver gelatin photograph with screen-printed text, 408 × 575 mm. Courtesy of The Mayor Gallery, London.*

shaving, bathing, even squeezing pimples might be art activities worth recording as such in photographic sequences. This threw into sharp relief the artificial nature of not only the art objects he was making, but also the art system itself. A regular choice for the important survey exhibition *Young Contemporaries,* he turned the tables in 1962 by entering a painting entitled *Young Contemporaries 1962* (1961), consisting entirely of an enlarged version of the entry blank for the exhibition itself. Bates then took a step taken by few other conceptualists. In his own words:

> In London in 1961 I began an extended work which was part of my effort to break down the separation between "life activity" and "art activity." I decided to use my own identity as a vehicle with which to explore the concept of the artist as an "art object." This began by changing my name (identification) and my

> physical appearance. Recreating myself became the art work. I relinquished my given name Barrie George Bates and chose the name Billy Apple to replace it. Then I assumed a new appearance which was Barrie Bates' conception of Billy Apple's image. At the home of Richard Smith, 13 Bath Street, London E.C. 1 in November 1962, I bleached my hair and my eyebrows yellow blonde with Lady Clairol Instant Creme Whip.[6]

In April 1963, Bates/Apple exhibited life-sized versions of his new passport photograph declaring his new identity. During the next few years he created works in various media—including bronze casts of apples and parts of his body, a pseudo-shop that sold "fruit"—punning on both his name and aspects of his identity-in-formation. Under the name Barrie Bates, he continued to show neon pieces in exhibitions in London and New York, where he moved in 1964. In October 1969, Apple opened a noncommercial space at 161 West 23rd Street, regularly showing installation and procedural pieces until it closed in June 1973. These included sweepings of roof dirt, collections of nasal and fecal matter over sustained periods, rubbish gatherings, destructions of glass tubing that were subsequently dispersed outside the city, and a number of actions that involved cleaning up specific spaces. Many other artists in New York and elsewhere were, at this time, also exploring such aspects of everyday life as art.

Ian Burn and Mel Ramsden met at the National Gallery School, Melbourne, in 1964. They both moved to London in 1965 and worked together on a daily basis, as they did after moving to New York in 1967 (their collaboration continued until 1977, when Burn moved to Sydney and Ramsden to England). In 1966 Ramsden made a number of *Untitled* paintings consisting of heavy black enamel surfaces mounted on deep stretchers of various shapes. There is reference here to Frank Stella's canvases of the late 1950s, regarded by many as the ultimate paintings, after which all that remained to painters was comment on this culmination. Ramsden's *Secret Painting* (1967–68), a black square shown alongside a statement to the effect that the work's content is known only to the artist, was part of a series labeled *Non-Visual Art*.

In 1965 Burn moved quickly from eccentric figuration in the manner of Sidney Nolan to colorfield works in which areas of color were generated by numbers and could be shifted in terms of positioning. He then did a series of "minimal"-style op paintings in which each work was repeated as a "proposition" about what a painting might be, for example,

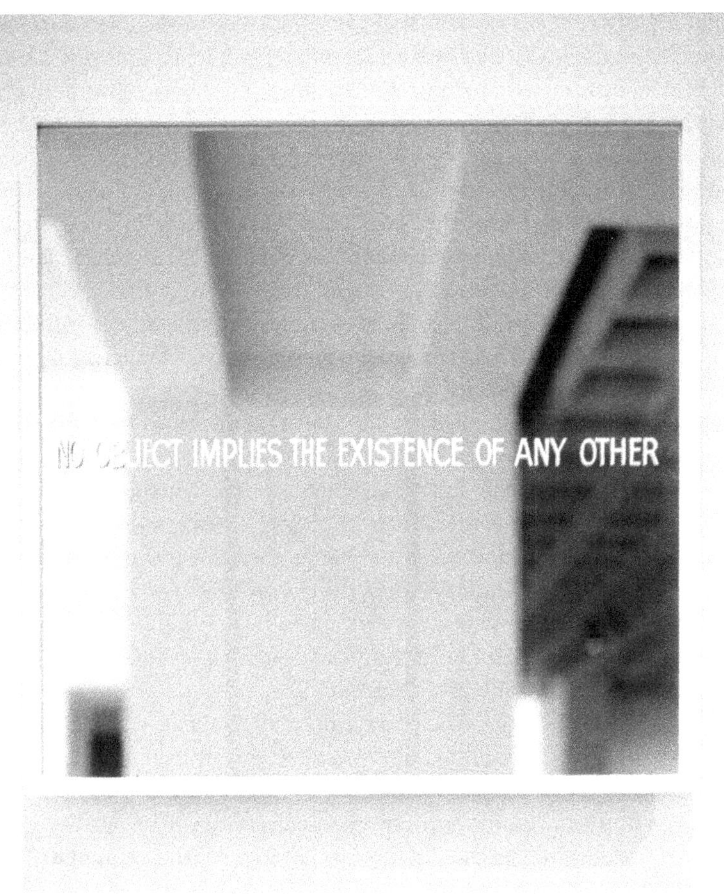

Ian Burn, No object implies the existence of any other, *1967.*
Synthetic polymer paint on wood, mirror, lettering, 64.5 × 64.5 × 3 cm.
Art Gallery of New South Wales, Rudy Komon Memorial Fund 1990.
Photo: AGNSW © Estate of Ian Burn 1317.1990.

the "six different exactly identical paintings" idea worked out as *Yellow Premiss* (1965). Burn then made a set of large minimal paintings of single colors painted with highly reflective enamels, followed by a series of *Mirror Pieces* (1967–68) in which the sequence of viewing was refracted by variations in the grinding, and thus reflectability, of the glass. These were soon accompanied by texts, framed and mounted alongside the painting, which discussed the materialities of the spectator's encounter, and increasingly, its phenomenology, for example, *No object implies the existence of any other* (1967).[7]

A little-known work that fully exemplifies this moment is *Soft-Tape* (1966) by Burn and Ramsden. Designed to be installed in a white room entirely empty except for a tape recorder on a white stand, the points raised by the piece were made explicit in a text displayed near the exit:

> Presentation of the work uses a taperecorder. The sound emitted by the recorder is kept throughout at a monotonous and uniform level which is (as near as possible) at the "zero-point" between understanding the spoken words and indecipherable noise. This is a means of stabilizing and holding directions at a point of "uncertainty"—which sets up the possibility of conflicting directions.
>
> Listening along a relaxed and "normal" sound level, it will appear that the recorded sound is a soft and even blur. This is intentional and any kind of variance (i.e. from the meaning of the words to the effect of the recorded sound) will be due to (i) the physical position of the spectator, or (ii) the amount of attention he is prepared to give. For this reason, other than the recorder mechanism, the display space is kept accessible and approach to the mechanism and its environs free.
>
> Instead of merely reproducing a standard symmetrical content, a framework of tension and possibility is set up between the spectator as receiver and the recorder as transmitter of the information. This is in order that the desired spatial "pattern" be achieved . . .
>
> ANY determining decisions a spectator makes while confronting the mechanism are to be considered a part of the intent of the piece.

This is John Cage without the silence, La Monte Young without the sound, Fluxus without the performance, but it is supplementary to all

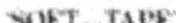

'SOFT—TAPE'

Presentation of the work uses a tape recorder. The sound emitted by the recorder is kept throughout at a monotonous and uniform level which is (as near as possible) at the 'zero-point' between understanding the spoken words and indecipherable noise. This is a means of stabilizing and holding directions at a point of 'uncertainty' – which sets up the possibility of conflicting directions.

Listening along a relaxed and 'normal' sound level, it will appear that the recorded sound is a soft and even blur. This is intentional and any kind of variance (i.e. from the *meaning* of the words to the *effect* of the recorded sound) will be due to (i) the physical position of the spectator, or (ii) the amount of attention he is prepared to give. For this reason, other than the recorder mechanism, the display space is kept accessible and approach to the mechanism and its environs free.

Instead of merely reproducing a standard symmetrical content, a framework of tension and possibility is set up between the spectator as receiver and the recorder as transmitter of the information. This is in order that the desired spatial 'pattern' be achieved.

The interpretation therefore is a matter for the spectator's own decisions and the kind of choices he makes in this respect will determine his understanding of the piece.

ANY determining decisions a spectator makes while confronting the mechanism are to be considered a part of the intent of the piece.

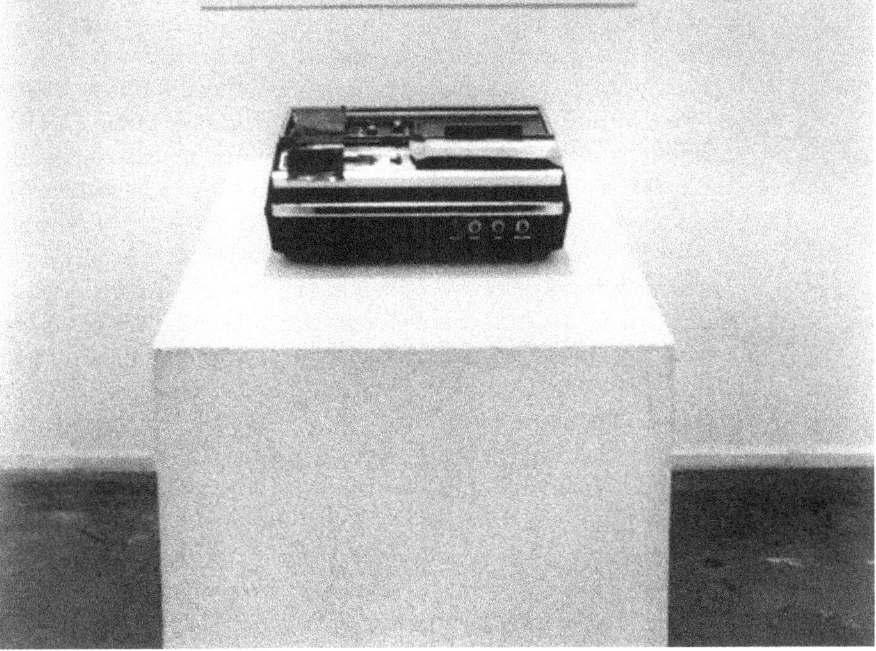

Ian Burn and Mel Ramsden, Soft-Tape, *1966. Tape recorder and photostat of wall notice. Courtesy Avril Burn and Mel Ramsden.*

of them, and to minimalism itself as a coalescing style. It was prepared for exhibition at Strines Gallery, Melbourne, a short-lived, avant-garde gallery specializing in presenting visual poems as artworks during the early 1960s. Concrete poetry, a small but active part of the widespread experimental poetry movement in Australia, was a pathway into conceptualism for artists such as Mike Parr.

Soft-Tape was not, in any event, shown in 1966, but the proposal circulated among artists in Australia, and Burn and Ramsden sought other opportunities for its realization, succeeding finally at the Sydney Biennale in 1990. Nevertheless, in this context, it is worth exploring the implications of its initial conceptualization, as this will take us to the heart of a certain emphasis in conceptualism's origins.

What kind of spectator did the two artists imagine? In the words spoken on the tape, they discuss a kind of art exemplified by *Soft-Tape* itself, an art that makes its "ideas" and "entire context" explicit. Since art objects are no longer capable of speaking for themselves, they must include words. Expressionist, sublime, heroic art is "simplistic"—instead, art should be "lucid." Art exists in space; indeed, space is created as the artwork is observed, read, understood. The "active participation" of the spectator, therefore, is highly valued; her behavior as an "auditor" determines the work. This should be done without changing the "tremendous fabric" of "light, space, time, materials, motion" that currently constitutes the world.

Shortly after the making of *Soft-Tape*, New York artist Lawrence Weiner called for a cessation of object making. In the aims and intentions expressed by Burn, Ramsden, and Weiner, there is a formidable challenge for art: to be about everything, but to be nothing in itself. This goes way beyond minimalism as a style, which even in its most radical forms remained a seductive reduction of previous sculpture. Nonintervention applied to the spectator as well. Is this the modernist spectator—much theorized in recent times by Jonathan Crary, Martin Jay, et al.—as the Cartesian Observer, the optical perceiver who sees the world in its entirety, who acts as a pure observing machine, that is, without changing the world in the process and without being changed in the process?[8]

In the stark directness with which it enacts the effort to understand pure spectatorship-in-process, *Soft-Tape* is a striking instance of conceptualism's concern with interrogating the relations between a perceiving subject and a perceived object. The words spoken on the tape itself, and the many notes written by Burn and Ramsden during October and November 1966 as they worked on the piece, demonstrate their acute awareness of these issues and how subtly they thought about them. It is obvious that they were fascinated with the idea of the imaginary spectator creating space by moving through time in the schematic room. In retrospect, another reading might be that *Soft-Tape* embodies the incommensurability at the base of cultural difference, that is, the great difficulties of understanding between cultures—in this case, art worlds. Hidden here is the germ of an idea that was to flower in the 1975 Art & Language exhibitions held in Melbourne and Adelaide (but not in Sydney).[9]

There are parallels here to events at the Coventry School of Art in 1965, where Michael Baldwin, working with Terry Atkinson, made a number of works consisting of mirrors mounted flush on stretchers, themselves wrapped in white canvas. Called *Untitled Paintings*, one was over life-size in height, very deep in frame, and installed hard up against a wall in the corner of a room. Another consisted of a set of four mirrors installed at usual viewing height for paintings. Meanwhile, in New York, Joseph Kosuth was seeking ways of interrogating minimalism's implications in a number of well-known works. This kind of shared background reinforced the collaboration between artists in the Art & Language group from 1969 onward for a number of years.[10] Burn and Ramsden continued to make art about the conditions of observation; by 1968, their work increasingly took the form of statements about these conditions, and then statements about the conditions of making these statements. This moves into what I would characterize as second-phase conceptualism. Works such as *Six Negatives* (1968–69) are entirely language-based. In 1969 Burn and Ramsden, with English artist Roger Cutforth, established the Society for Theoretical Art and Analyses. Later that year they began to contribute to *Art-Language*, the "journal of conceptual art" produced by the British-based Art & Language group, which they joined formally in 1971. Richard Dunn, another Australian who traveled through minimal painting and installations, arrived—during his expatriate time—at similar works, for example, *The Art.Act* (1969).[11]

AROUND 1970: RUPTURE AND NEXUS

As conceptualism increased in intensity and diversity during the later 1960s and early 1970s, and as it became an evident international style, it affected one practicing generation of Australian avant-garde painters and sculptors as a massively debilitating force while at the same time liberating another. Accomplished and subtle minimal painters such as Robert Jacks, Dale Hickey, Robert Hunter, and Paul Partos—all of whom went to New York during the moment of conceptualism's greatest

Mike Parr, Wall Definition, *1971. 254 A4 typed pages. Collection of the artist. Courtesy the artist and Anna Schwartz Gallery.*

impact—were traumatized. Their return to Melbourne in the mid-1970s meant an extremely tentative return to painting, one that only very slowly recovered its strength.[12]

In contrast, a younger generation of Australian and New Zealand artists responded positively to magazine-circulated information about the range of Conceptual Art, Arte Povera, performance, land art, earthworks, installation art, etc., being made around the world at the time. *Studio International* was influential in the region, as was an essay by Ian Burn, "Conceptual Art as Art," published in the standard journal *Art and Australia* in September 1970. In Sydney, critic Donald Brook actively promoted what he called "post-object art," while in New Zealand, writer Wystan Curnow argued strongly for the "new art."[13] This mix engendered an array of conceptual practices that quickly came to lead artmaking in the region in the early 1970s.

One tendency was language-based work such as Mike Parr's *Wall Definition* (1971), consisting of 254 quarto pages on which the *Oxford English Dictionary* definition of the word *wall* was typed out again and again. Work on this project led Parr to recognize the implications of autism as a metaphor for the limitations of self-knowledge.[14] But despite the prominence of language in the art of the region—including

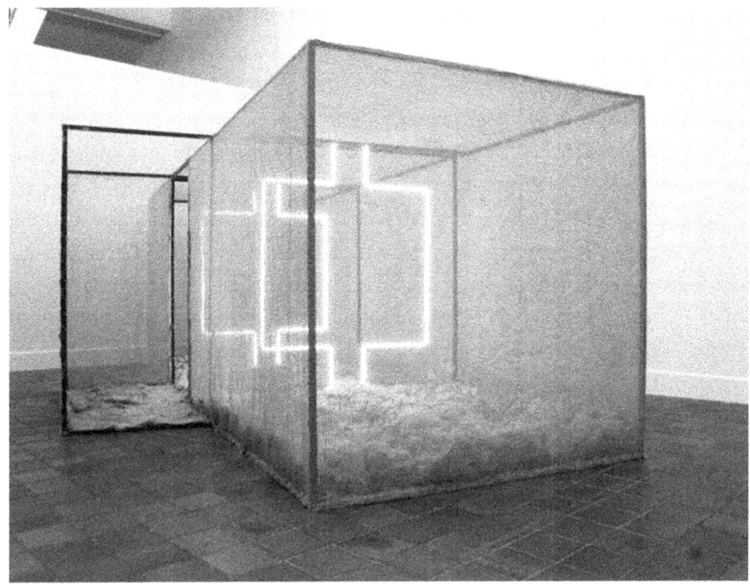

Jim Allen, New Zealand Environment No. 5, *1969. Scrim, steel tube, greasy wool, sawdust, underfelt, barbed wire, and neon. Courtesy Govett-Brewster Art Gallery, New Plymouth, New Zealand.*

the citation of ritual song and sign in the work of Maori artists—it was seldom used by New Zealand conceptualists as the form of the work. One rare example is Nicholas Spill's series of images of milk spilling through words such as *milk*, obviously punning on his own name.

Funky, ironic, parodic approaches to conceptual issues are another distinctive local tendency in these years. *Walk Along This Line* (1971) by Ian Milliss consisted of a strip of masking tape laid so close to a wall that anyone following the instruction would fall over. Aleks Danko's *Auto Realism* (1971), a mirror piece with its title engraved in the glass, framed the viewer's reflected face. Robert Rooney carefully photographed his folded clothes laid out on his bed each night for over three months in *Garments: 3 December 1972 to 19 March 1973*, one of a series of studies on suburban rituals.

A third major tendency was the tracing of processes as they applied to bodies, objects, and spaces. A pathbreaking example in New Zealand was Jim Allen's *New Zealand Environment No. 5* (1969), a sequence of rooms in which the unalloyed experience of various textures—including steel, greasy wool, sawdust, underfelt, and barbed wire—was possible for the person seeking "pure" tactility. In the virtual absence of emphasis on visuality, there is a strange parallel here to the auditory emphasis of *Soft-Tape*. The artist-run Inhibodress Gallery in Sydney was a center for experimental art that tested the limits of both communication and audience empathy in works setting propositions against bodies, objects, spaces. Founders Peter Kennedy and Mike Parr performed many actions under the heading *Trans Art*, particularly those exploring extremes of pain. These are recorded in the 1972 film by Aggy Read and Ian Stocks, *Idea Demonstrations*. Also at Inhibodress, Tim Johnson displayed the photographic record of voyeuristic actions conducted in public, entitled *Disclosures* (1972).[15]

Sound as a delineator of space interested Peter Kennedy in pieces such as *But the Fierce Blackman* (1972), in which the phrase "But the fierce blackman . . ." was repeated and played at varying levels through speakers set out in a staged location in the gallery. Philip Dadson worked in Cornelius Cardew's Scratch Orchestra in London in 1968, and founded the New Zealand Scratch Orchestra in 1970, an offshoot of which—From Scratch—still performs today. At 1800 hours Greenwich Mean Time on September 23 and 24, 1971, fifteen groups of people at Dadson's behest recorded the circumstances of that exact moment in fifteen locations around the world. This was his *Earthworks*, existing now as a photographic map and film record.

MID-1970s

Conceptual practices all over the world turned—or, in many cases, returned—to socially embedded work in the early 1970s. This was, in part, a reaction against conceptualism becoming Conceptual Art. It was also a result of the dire social and political situation in most countries during the late 1960s, which could no longer be acknowledged by an equivalent or indirect artistic radicalism. Australian conceptualism was slow to respond for quite local reasons: in 1972 the Labor Party became the federal government for the first time in nearly twenty years, and along with its radical social agenda came a liberatory and internationalizing cultural policy, including the establishment of significant support for experimental art. The Labor government was dismissed from office by the Queen's representative in 1975, and the instantly intensified political climate prompted some activity among conceptual artists, for example, the Provisional Art & Language exhibitions in Melbourne, Adelaide, and Auckland in 1975–76, which addressed questions of provin-

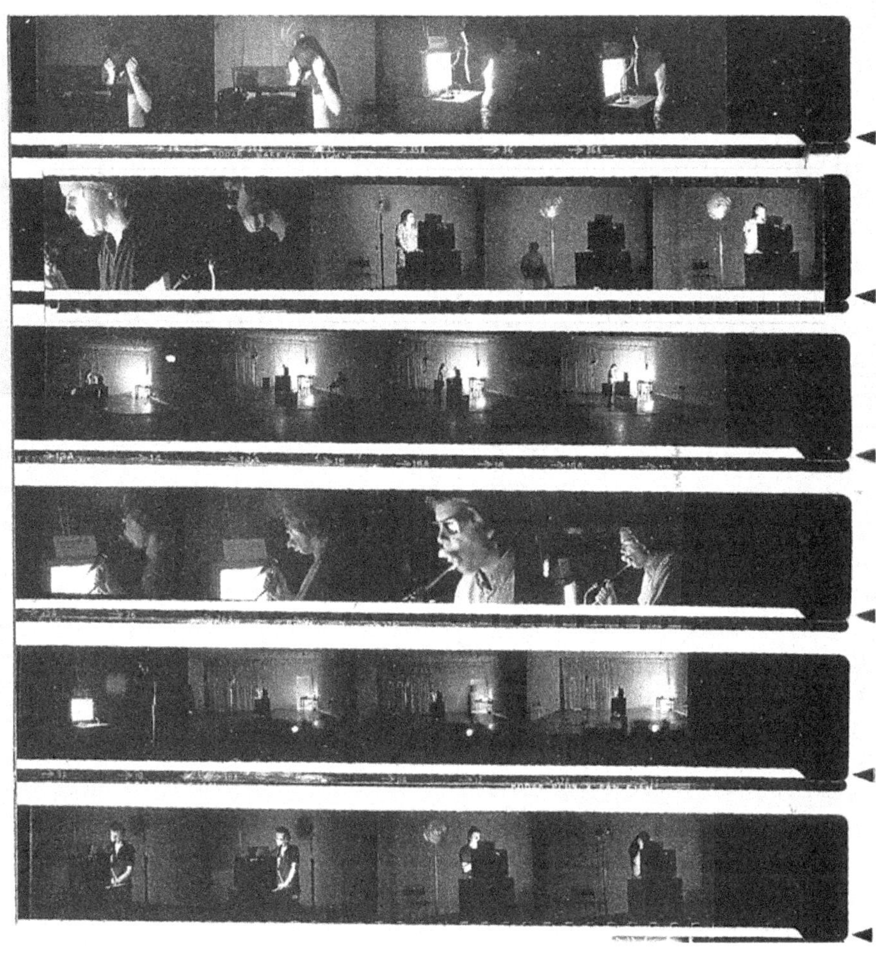

Peter Kennedy, But the Fierce Blackman, *1972. Sound performance. Courtesy the artist and Milani Gallery, Brisbane.*

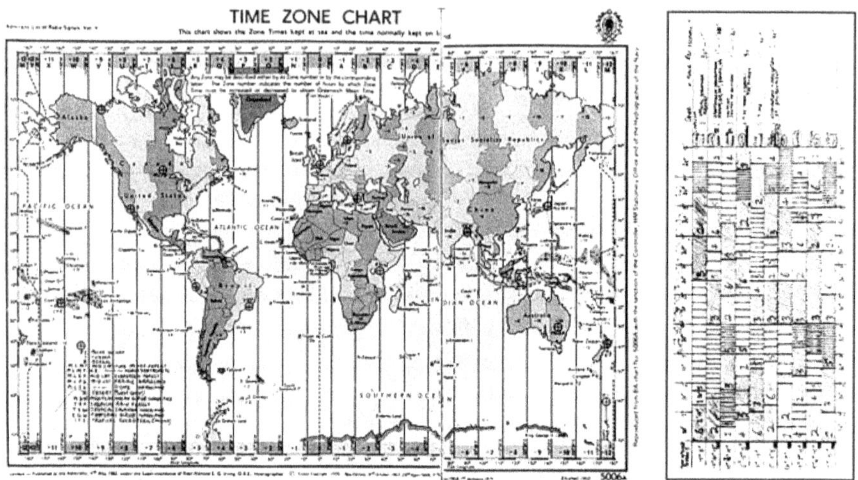

Philip Dadson, Earthworks—Timezone Map of the World, *1971.*
Color map mounted on stiff board. Collection of the artist.

cialism and cultural imperialism in provocative ways. Two were closed by state governments.[16]

Another relevant development of the mid-1970s was the emergence of isolated rereadings of key currents of early avant-garde modernism. These include Imants Tillers's *Moments of Inertia* (1972–73), John Nixon's *Self-Portrait (Non-Objective Composition)* series (begun 1975), and Peter Tyndall's *detail: A Person Looks At A Work Of Art/someone looks at something* series (begun 1974). Tyndall's work returns the gaze of the Cartesian spectator by showing every viewer an impossibly generalized, humorously reduced figure of him- or herself. The specifically local take of these projects is their parodic exaggeration of the fact that provincial art cultures learn their structures of belief and their visual repertoires from reproduced images and ideas that have originated elsewhere. And then they strive to turn this adopted currency into an expressive practice.

LEGACIES

"Post-conceptual painting" is a term that I have used to designate the main tendency in Australian art during the 1980s. Its most prominent practitioners include Juan Davila, Mike Parr, Imants Tillers, and Susan Norrie. They are all artists whose medium may be painting of one kind or another but whose content concerns the most important questions of identity and alterity, and whose aesthetic is one that makes perception itself a complex provisionality.[17]

Since the early 1970s, Indigenous artists have developed and sustained an art movement matching post-conceptualism as the other main current in Australian art. While Aboriginal artists living in traditional communities have shown little interest in Conceptual Art, certain artists of Aboriginal background whose experience has been formed in predominantly non-Indigenous settings (including art schools much concerned with postmodernism) have drawn on conceptualism in striking ways. Gordon Bennett's six-panel piece *Untitled* (1989) uses a string of nominations typical of propositional Conceptual Art to underscore the impact of European possession of Terra Australis.[18] Conceptual procedures also resonate in the work of Tracey Moffatt, Destiny Deacon, Fiona Foley, and others. Maori artists seem not to have drawn on the conceptual-minimal legacy to quite the same extent.

During the 1990s, a further generation of younger artists, responding in part to the above developments and to Metro Pictures–type neoconceptualism, have developed a wide-ranging and subtle array of conceptual-minimal work.[19] They are part of the conceptual-minimal nexus forged in the years around 1970, the legacy of which still shapes advanced art in Australia and New Zealand today.

NOTES

This chapter was originally published as Terry Smith, "Peripheries in Motion: Conceptualism and Conceptual Art in Australia and New Zealand," in Luis Camnitzer, Jane Farver, and Rachael Weiss, eds., Global Conceptualism: Points of Origin, 1950s–1980s *(New York: Queens Museum of Art, 1999), 87–95.*

1. General texts include Bernard Smith with Terry Smith, *Australian Painting, 1788 to 1990* (Melbourne: Oxford University Press, 1991); Christopher Allen, *Art in Australia* (London: Thames and Hudson, 1997); Gil Docking, *Two Hundred Years of New Zealand Painting*, 2nd ed. (Glenfield, New Zealand: Bateman, 1990); Anne Kirker, *New Zealand Women Artists: A Survey of 150 Years* (Tortola, Virgin Islands: Craftsman House, 1993).

2. See Margaret Plant, *Irreverent Sculpture* (Melbourne: Monash University Art Gallery, 1985), and the entry "Annandale Imitation Realists," in Jane Turner, ed., *Dictionary of Art*, vol. 2 (London: Macmillan, 1996), 120.

3. See Smith with Smith, *Australian Painting*, chapter 13 for Central

Street, and Sue Cramer, *Inhibodress* (Brisbane, Australia: Museum of Modern Art, 1989).

4. This is explored in the Australian context in my interview with Jelena Stojanovic, "Conceptual Art Then and Since," *Agenda Contemporary Art Magazine* 26 (November–December 1992) and 27 (January–February 1993), supplement.

5. See the essay by Lawrence Alloway in Lucy R. Lippard, ed., *Pop Art* (New York: Praeger, 1966).

6. Quoted in Arts Council of Great Britain, *From Barrie Bates to Billy Apple, 1960–1974* (London: Serpentine Gallery, 1974), 11. It is notable that David Hockney (like Andy Warhol) presented himself at this time with bleached hair, but not himself as a work of art.

7. Ian Burn, *Minimal-Conceptual Work, 1965–1970* (Perth: Art Gallery of Western Australia, 1992).

8. Jonathan Crary, *Techniques of the Observer* (Cambridge, MA: MIT Press, 1990); Martin Jay, *Downcast Eyes: The Denigration of Vision in Twentieth-Century French Thought* (Berkeley: University of California Press, 1994).

9. Terry Smith, ed., *Art & Language: Australia 1975* (Banbury, UK: Art & Language Press, 1975).

10. See Charles Harrison, *Essays on Art and Language* (Oxford: Blackwell, 1991).

11. See *Richard Dunn: The Dialectical Image: Selected Work, 1964–1992* (Sydney: Art Gallery of New South Wales, 1992).

12. Smith with Smith, *Australian Painting*, chapter 14.

13. Donald Brook, "Flight from the Object," in Bernard Smith, ed., *Concerning Contemporary Art* (Oxford: Clarendon, 1975). See also Terry Smith and Paul McGillick, *The Situation Now: Object or Post-Object Art?* (Sydney: Contemporary Art Society, 1971), and Jim Allen and Wystan Curnow, *New Art: Some Recent New Zealand Sculpture and Post-Object Art* (Auckland, New Zealand: Heinemann, 1976).

14. See David Bromfield, *Identities: A Critical Study of the Works of Mike Parr, 1970–1990* (Nedlands: University of Western Australia Press, 1991).

15. See Cramer, *Inhibodress*, and Anne Marsh, *Body and Self: Performance Art in Australia, 1969–1992* (Melbourne: Oxford University Press, 1993).

16. See Terry Smith, "The Tasks of Translation: Art & Language in Australia and New Zealand 1975–6," in Ian Wedde and Gregory Burke, eds., *Now See Hear! Art, Language, and Translation* (Wellington, New Zealand: Victoria University Press, 1990).

17. Smith with Smith, *Australian Painting*, chapter 16.

18. Ian Mclean, *The Art of Gordon Bennett* (Roseville East, NSW: Craftsman House, 1996).

19. See Smith, "Conceptual Art Then and Since," and Charles Green, *Peripheral Vision: Contemporary Australian Art, 1970–1994* (Roseville East, NSW: Craftsman House, 1995).

One and Three Ideas

Conceptualism Before, During, and After Conceptual Art

5

Tactically, conceptualism is no doubt the strongest position of the three; for the tired nominalist can lapse into conceptualism and still allay his puritanic conscience with the reflection that he has not quite taken to eating lotus with the Platonists.

Willard van Orman Quine

Philosophers often add "-ism" to a term in order to highlight a distinct approach to a fundamental question, that is, to name a philosophical doctrine. For example, when it comes to universals, *The Oxford Dictionary of Philosophy* tells us that "conceptualism is a doctrine in philosophy intermediate between nominalism and realism that says universals exist only within the mind and have no external or substantial reality."[1] There are other definitions, but the point about the use of "-ism" to name a philosophical doctrine is clear. For art critics, curators, and historians, however, "-isms" have somewhat different purposes: they name movements in art, broadly shared approaches that have become styles or threaten to do so. During the heroic years of the modern movement, when critics, artists, or art historians first added "-ism" to a word, they usually meant what the suffix usually means in ordinary language: that *x* is like *y*, even excessively so. Often with ridicule as their aim, they highlighted a quality twice removed from the source of that particular art, from its authenticity. Thus "Impressionism" and "Cubism," neither of which names what is really going on in the art to which it refers: each takes up a banal misdescription and then exaggerates it into a ludicrous delusion on the part of the artists. The success of the early twentieth-century avant-gardes led to a plethora of "-isms" that gradually lost these negative connotations and become almost normal descriptors. By midcentury, anyone could generate an "-ism," and too many artists did so in their efforts to link their unique, often quite individual ways of making art to what they, or their promoters, hoped would be market success and art-historical inevitability. When Willem de Kooning, at a meeting of artists in New York in 1951, said, "It is disastrous to name ourselves," his was a lone voice, quickly silenced by the tide that named all present Abstract Expressionists.

By the 1960s this kind of naming had become so commonplace, so obvious a move, and such a sure pathway to premature institutionalization and incorporation, that many artists rejected it, to avoid being comfortably slotted into what they regarded as an ossified history of modernist avant-gardism. In the 1970s, for example, artists driven primarily by political concerns consciously blocked efforts to designate their work as belonging to a "political art" movement. Yet for some artists, long excluded from any kind of historical recognition, this was a risk worth taking: feminist artists emphasized their feminism, for instance, precisely because it connected their practice to the broader social movement to vindicate the rights of women.

As the artists most acutely aware of the powers and the pitfalls of exactly these processes, conceptual artists refused to embrace the term "conceptualism" during the 1960s, '70s, and '80s. They were, however, happy to use terms such as "conceptual" for their work, because questioning the concept of art was precisely the main point of their practice. As we shall see, they foresaw that the tag "Conceptual Art" would inevitably be associated with their work, and thus tie it too closely to art that had already resolved its problems. Their goal was to keep their art (practice) problematic to themselves by keeping it at a (critical) distance from Art (as an institution). They therefore sought to prevent the precipitous labeling of their art by adopting one or both of two strategies: insist that the term "conceptual" be applied so broadly (describing any art no longer governed by a traditional medium) as to be meaningless, or so narrowly (indicating only language-based art that dealt with Art per se) as to be offensive to almost everyone.

It is a nice paradox that the term "conceptualism" came into art-world existence after the advent of Conceptual Art in major centers such as New York and London—most prominently and programmatically in the exhibition *Global Conceptualism: Points of Origin, 1950s–1980s* at the Queens Museum of Art in New York in 1999—mainly in order to highlight the fact that innovative, experimental art practices occurred in the Soviet Union, Japan, South America, and elsewhere prior to, at the same time as, and after the European and U.S. initiatives that had come to seem paradigmatic, and to claim that these practices were more socially and politically engaged—and thus more relevant to their present, better models for today's art, and, in these senses, better art—than the well-known Euro-American exemplars. I explored a variant of this idea—that conceptualism was an outcome of some artists' increased global mobility—in my selections for the *Global Conceptualism* exhibition, and in my catalog essay, "Peripheries in Motion: Conceptualism and Conceptual Art in Australia and New Zealand."[2] Retrospection of this kind has also shone spotlights on what were once regarded as minor movements in Euro-American art (Fluxus, for example).

The question posed by the exhibition *Traffic: Conceptual Art in Canada 1965–1980*, presented at the University of Toronto Art Galleries in 2010, is whether a similar valuing structure might be applied to certain strands in art made in Canada from the 1960s to the present. Even though Canadian artists were conspicuously absent from *Global Conceptualism*, certain artists have since been valued as contributors to the international tendency. Thus the exhibition asks us to look in more detail at work of the time made throughout the regions of Canada and consider whether perhaps this valuing can be extended to them. There is no suggestion that this art was nationalistic—on the contrary, it was everywhere based on skepticism about official national culture-construction. The implication is that regional conceptualisms existed—that is, that conceptualist developments (in the broadest sense) occurred differently in each of the distinct regions of Canada. Again, the implication is skeptical: in every case it is about regionality in transition, not a self-satisfied parochialism.

Triggered by remarks made by some of the key artists back in the day, I wish to revisit the terms "Conceptual Art" and "conceptualism" as indications of what was at stake in the unraveling of late modern art during the 1960s and in art's embrace of contemporaneity since. I will do so by asking what conceptualism was before, during, and after Conceptual Art, and I will show that there were at least one, usually two, and sometimes three conceptions of conceptualism in play at each moment—and that these were in play, differently although connectedly, in various places, at each of these times.

POP OR CONCEPTUAL? OR BOTH AND NEITHER?

Let me begin with the question as seen from within orthodox art historical narratives, as a matter of the meaning of style, a concern of art historians. I start from before Conceptual Art was named as a style, before the term "conceptualism" had any currency, to see what might count as Conceptual Art in that circumstance.

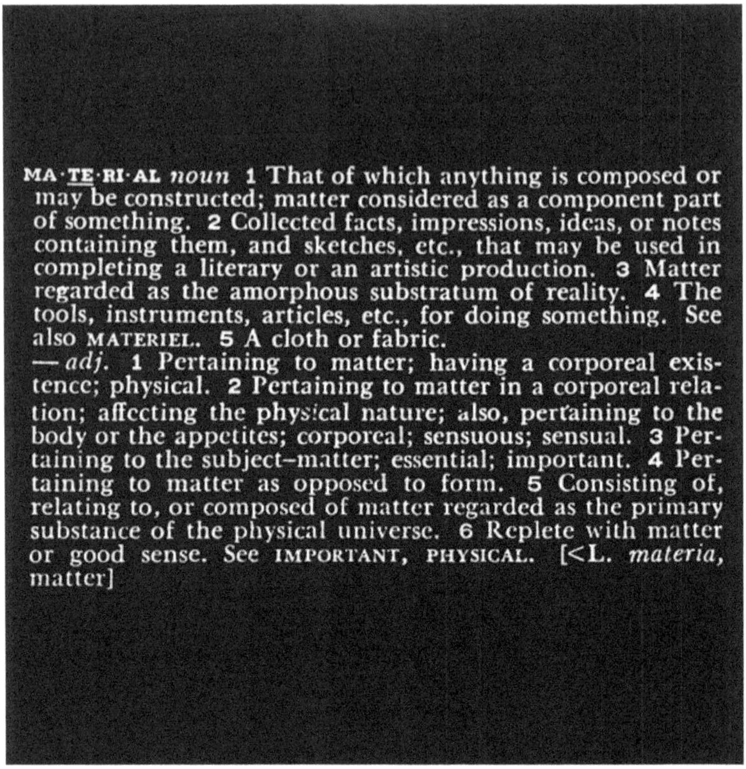

MA·TE·RI·AL *noun* 1 That of which anything is composed or may be constructed; matter considered as a component part of something. 2 Collected facts, impressions, ideas, or notes containing them, and sketches, etc., that may be used in completing a literary or an artistic production. 3 Matter regarded as the amorphous substratum of reality. 4 The tools, instruments, articles, etc., for doing something. See also MATERIEL. 5 A cloth or fabric.
—*adj.* 1 Pertaining to matter; having a corporeal existence; physical. 2 Pertaining to matter in a corporeal relation; affecting the physical nature; also, pertaining to the body or the appetites; corporeal; sensuous; sensual. 3 Pertaining to the subject-matter; essential; important. 4 Pertaining to matter as opposed to form. 5 Consisting of, relating to, or composed of matter regarded as the primary substance of the physical universe. 6 Replete with matter or good sense. See IMPORTANT, PHYSICAL. [<L. *materia*, matter]

Joseph Kosuth, Art as Idea as Idea (Material), *1968. Photostat on paper mounted on wood. Private collection, Pittsburgh.*

Ian Burn, in conversation in late 1972, said of Joseph Kosuth's *Art as Idea* works: "If they were made in 1965 like he claims, they are Pop Art. If they were made in 1967–8, when they were exhibited, then they are among the first conceptual works, strictly speaking." In his 1970 essay "Conceptual Art as Art," Burn gave these works this latter dating and characterized them as key examples of the "strict form of Conceptual Art" because they were analytic of the nature of art, their (minimal) appearance being of the most minimal relevance.[3] Why did an artist with such a critical attitude toward orthodox art history's puerile dependence on style terms apply such crude criteria to the work of a close colleague?[4]

Kosuth's response was outrage at applying such anti-conceptual criteria to such work: he was an art student who had the ideas but not the resources to realize them; by the time he did have these resources a few years later, everyone (including Burn) was dating their work to the moment of conception—immediacy was the new currency.[5]

In one sense Kosuth's *One and Three Chairs* (1965) is Pop-like in that its statement about what constitutes a sign is all there, all at once, and obvious, as in your face as Richard Hamilton's 1956 collage *Just what is it that makes today's homes so different, so appealing?*, but without the fascinated irony that informs the British artist's perspective. To an observer outside the U.S. sphere of cultural influence—or, more accurately, at its waxing and waning borders—*One and Three Chairs* might seem to offer viewers an open choice as to which item seems the most attractive constituent of "chairness," thereby reducing spectatorship to supermarket-like art consumption, and artmaking to the provision of competitive goods.[6] To the extent that this is true, Conceptual Art that turns on overt demonstration or the instantiation of an idea (as does much of the better-known and easily illustrated work—think Baldessari, Acconci, or Huebler) shares something with what might be called ordinary language Pop art, that which recycles the visual codes of consumer culture.

But the matter does not end there. In my view, the invitation to look in *One and Three Chairs* is at least as subtle as it is in key works on this subject by Rauschenberg, Johns, and Warhol in its conceptual questioning of what it is to see, what an image might be, what an idea looks like. These artists regularly juxtaposed photographs and objects such as actual chairs (in Rauschenberg's *Pilgrim*, for example), or evoked black-and-white photography and overtly displayed the tools that made them (Johns's *Periscope (Hart Crane)*, 1963, for example). Warhol's *Dance Diagram ("The Lindy Tuck-In Turn-Man")*, 1963, is an appropriation of an illustration, but it is also a demonstration of what constitutes a visual sign, especially when displayed, as he preferred, on the floor. Indeed, Warhol now seems the most nakedly conceptual of artists (in this pre–Conceptual Art moment), precisely in his instinct for setting out one visual idea at a time, in showing an image as an idea, in making artworks that plainly demonstrated how visual ideas achieved appearance in the culture, in the visual culture, in popular imagination, in unArt, in America. The idea-image, for him, was in David Antin's brilliant perception, a "deteriorated image."[7]

There were, of course, many others striving to picture the many dichotomies afforded by the idea-image interplay that was taking shape at the time: a random list must include Guy Debord, with his films such

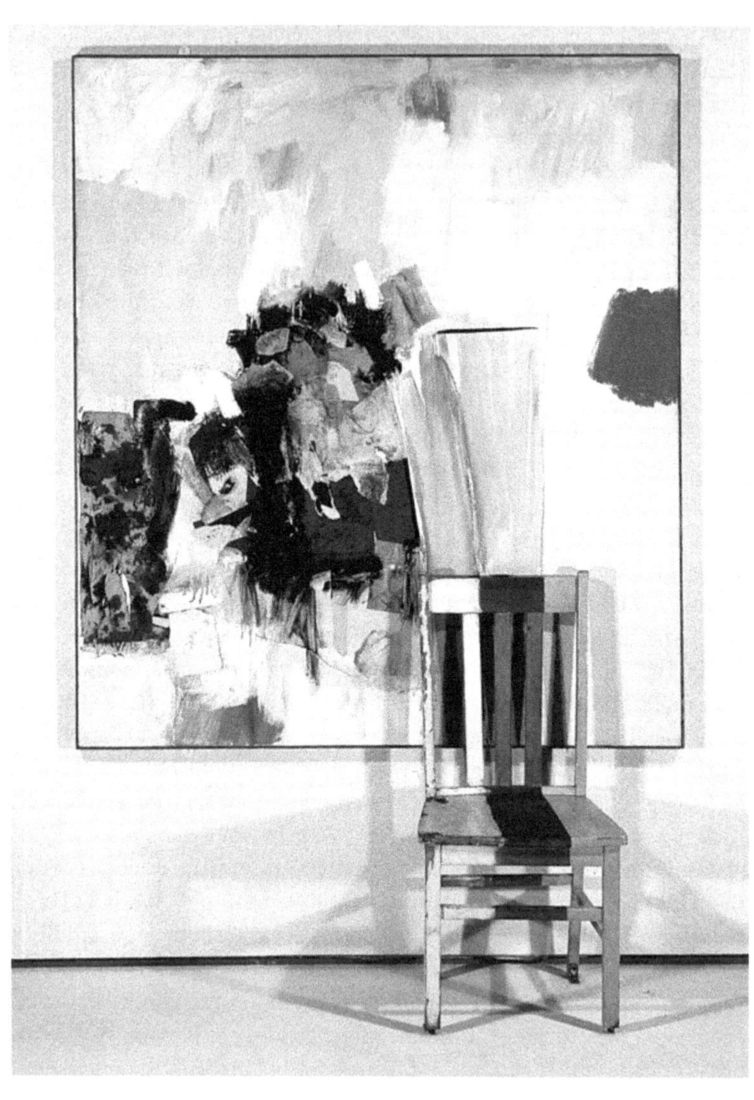

Robert Rauschenberg, Pilgrim, *1960. Combine: oil, graphite, paper, printed paper, and fabric on canvas with painted wood chair, 79¼ × 53⅞ × 18⅝ inches (201.3 × 136.8 × 47.3 cm). Onnasch Collection.*

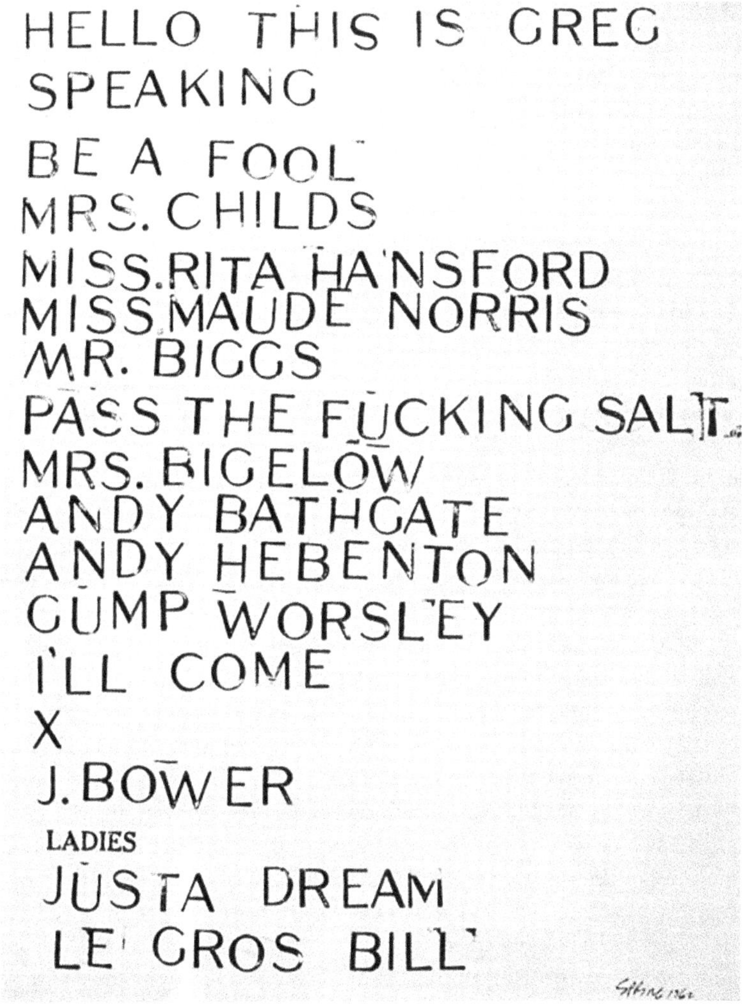

HELLO THIS IS GREG
SPEAKING
BE A FOOL
MRS. CHILDS
MISS. RITA HANSFORD
MISS MAUDE NORRIS
MR. BIGGS
PASS THE FUCKING SALT
MRS. BIGELOW
ANDY BATHGATE
ANDY HEBENTON
GUMP WORSLEY
I'LL COME
X
J. BOWER
LADIES
JUST A DREAM
LE GROS BILL

Greg Curnoe, Row of Words on My Mind #1, *1962. Stamp pad, ink.*
Image courtesy of the CCCA Canadian Art Database.

as *Hurlements en faveur de Sade* (1952) and his collaborations with Asger Jorn; concrete poets of all kinds; Jim Dine; Kaprow, with his early happenings; Ed Ruscha; and many others, all of whom converge with Pop in certain ways, although they, like the artists mentioned above, were on a track much more interesting than that which can be encompassed by that term. In Canada, Greg Curnoe's work throughout the 1960s offers a fascinating instance of a figurative painter, alert to the stylistics of Pop and flat color abstraction, yet, like Kurt Schwitters, drawn irresistibly to the potency of words and texts as they occur in the flow and stuff of everyday life. Add to this a Wittgensteinian consciousness that we are all products of our language-worlds, and an interesting outcome is assured. Thus, in *Westing House Workers* (1962), the names of a group of laborers are stamped out on a sheet that seems taken from a factory cafeteria notice board, while *Row of Words on My Mind #1* (1962) stamps out a set of names of people, things, promises, and so forth, that seem as random as anyone's everyday ruminations. By 1967, however, Curnoe had evidently seen tautology-based conceptualism (either through reproductions or via the agency of Greg Ferguson): *Front Center Windows* (1967) is a blue vertical rectangle stamped with black letters that describe a façade in the language of a builder's report, while *Non-Figurative Picture* (1968) is a vertical column stamped with the letters of the alphabet.

These examples tell us that the question "Is it Pop or Conceptual Art?" is at best a provocation (as it was for Burn), and at worst a badly formulated misunderstanding of the deeper stakes of both kinds of work. Rather, we can see that various kinds of conceptualization inspired the most inventive artists of the late modern era and that the conceptual qualities of their work were among its most important. This is the first, the most rooted, sense in which the three ideas of what it is for art to be conceptual could count as one idea: the term "conceptual" as an adjective is most fitting to this sense. Quite properly, this basic usage precedes any real usage of the terms "conceptualism" and "Conceptual Art" in art discourse, as these are derivative from it. It permits us this proposition, the first part of a proposal that I advance—with full awareness of how paradoxical a gesture it is—as "a theory of conceptualism":

1. At its various beginnings, conceptualism was a set of practices for interrogating what it was for perceiving subjects and perceived objects to be in the world (that is, it was an inquiry into the minimal situations in which art might be possible).[8]

A WORK OF ART BECOMES CONSEQUENTIAL WHEN IT COUNTS AS ART

It is lazy-mindedness to say that all art that evidently reflects on its own medium, that does so in ways unusual enough to raise the question "Is this art?," qualifies as conceptual? There is a widespread sense, in today's sloppy art babble, that any art that has resulted from the artist having any kind of idea is "conceptual." Not so. You have to show that particular works, or groups of works, or a set of protocols, or a practice did these things consciously as opposed to by instinct, intelligently as distinct from intuitively, and did so effectively, with impact, with consequence.

On a number of occasions in conversation, Joseph Kosuth has pooh-poohed as pure pedantry my referencing Henry Flynt's use of the term "Concept Art" in 1961, despite the fact that it is the first documented usage in an art context.[9] "Who was this Flynt? A nobody. Who heard him, who knew of him, who cared what he said? So what if some thirteenth-century Chinese painter threw ink around in ways that look Pollock-like, or that Max Ernst did?" To Kosuth, what counts is not who said what when as a matter of plain record, or what was done in some isolated, adventitious circumstance, but whether the utterance, the work, the proposition counted in the dominant art discourse of the time. This alerts us to the internal struggle, among artists, critics, and theorists—that is, within art discourse itself—as to what was at stake in Conceptual Art and conceptualism as practices of art.

Thus Kosuth's famous statement, in "Art after Philosophy," that "all art (after Duchamp) is conceptual (in nature) because art only exists conceptually" is not to be taken to mean that all art influenced by Duchampian strategies is conceptual, and that other art is some other kind of art. It means that only Duchampian art is truly art, and that other art is not art precisely because it does not take on the challenge of framing new propositions about art and as art.[10]

From this perspective, Robert Morris has a much stronger claim to consequence in works such as *Card File* (1962): these overtly pit the complexity of his actual life and self against the limited information contained in official descriptions of a person. Two *Untitled* works of 1962 (recently added to MoMA's collection) are nothing more, but no less, than gray gouache painted over sheets of newspaper to the point of nearly obliterating the images and text. But did Morris go on with this particular line of inquiry? A short answer would be that it became one of

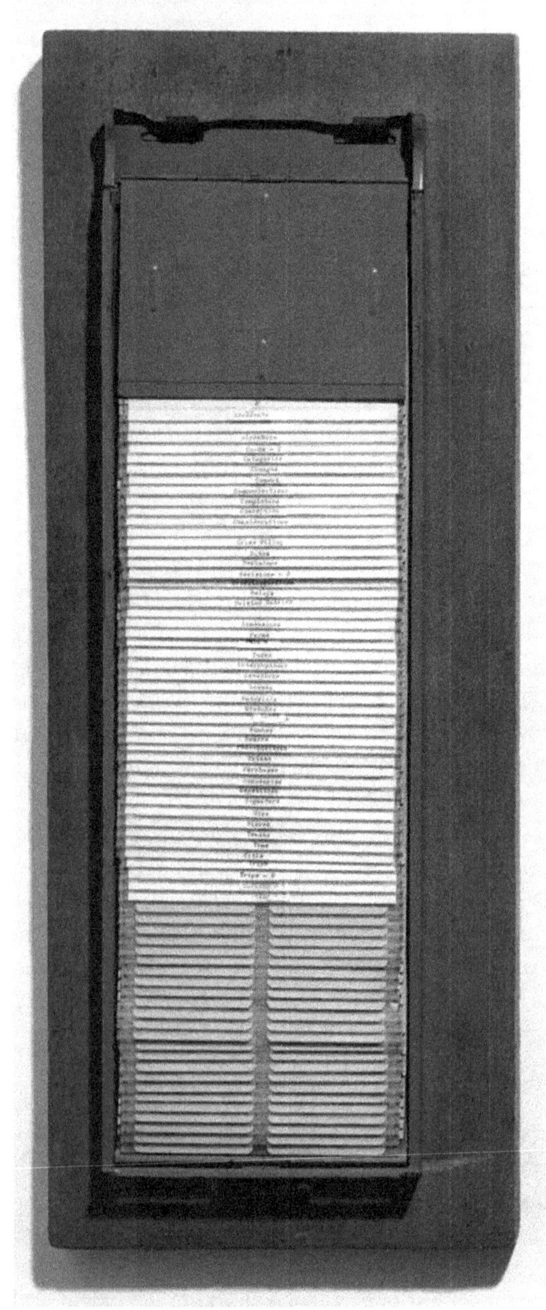

Robert Morris, Card File, *July 11–December 31, 1962. Metal, paper; 68.5 × 27 × 4 cm. Photo: Philippe Migeat © CNAC/MNAM/Dist. RMN-Grand Palais/Art Resource, NY/Artists Rights Society (ARS), NY.*

the many lines that he has since pursued, but a longer answer is needed to do justice to such a profound *oeuvre*.[11]

In Poland, Roman Opałka began his "infinity" paintings in 1965, sizing them to his studio doorway, beside which he has had himself photographed as each one is completed. On Kawara began traveling the world and sending daily postcards in 1959, then started making a date painting every day in 1966, and two years later embarked on the production of his *One-Hundred Year Calendar* that lists everyone he meets each day. Examples of such total commitment to applying a routine to a life, knowing that the two are fundamentally incompatible, abound. They may be found all over the world during this period and are constantly being taken up nowadays by young artists (Emese Benczúr, for example). I think that we are getting close to the core of conceptualism worthy of the name and to the basis of its appeal to serious young artists today: it is something to do with rigor, without cause, and with implacable commitment in the face of meaninglessness. So, in retrospect, it is no surprise that such a spirit should emerge from within the conflicted confusions of the mid- and later 1960s.

Sol LeWitt's statement, in his 1967 "Paragraphs on Conceptual Art," is famous:

> In conceptual art the idea or concept is the most important aspect of the work. When an artist uses a conceptual form of art, it means that all of the planning and decisions are made beforehand and the execution is a perfunctory affair. The idea becomes a machine that makes the art.[12]

This seems clear to the point of being classical (indeed, the last sentence is one of the epigrams to "Art after Philosophy"). But we need to ask: what did LeWitt mean by "the idea or concept"? If one examines closely the nature of these paragraphs, as an artist's statement—that is, if you put them back into the context of his own practice and see them as first and foremost a statement of the principles governing *that* practice (not all possible practice, not the practice most desired of all artists from now on)—then it becomes obvious that what LeWitt meant by an idea was a geometrical figure, and what he meant by a concept was a procedure for carrying out the realization of this idea, for example, as a singularity or as a specified sequence.

If, however, you read closely the 1969 "Sentences on Conceptual Art" (copies of the handwritten and corrected versions of 1968 have recently come to light), you are immediately thrown into the paradox just mentioned:

1. Conceptual artists are mystics rather than rationalists. They leap to conclusions that logic cannot reach.
2. Rational judgments repeat rational judgments.
3. Irrational judgments lead to new experience.
4. Formal art is essentially rational.
5. Irrational thoughts should be followed absolutely and logically.[13]

The contrast between rationality and mysticism is weak, and soon disappears. More important is that here we can see awareness of the reach but also the limits of ideas and concepts narrowly defined. It is their potential to create chaos, disorder, and revolution that comes to be valued, thus the peculiar poignancy of the proposals from visiting artists—to be realized by students, and, occasionally, the artists themselves—in David Askevold's Projects Class at NSCAD from 1969 forward. The postcards of the instructions, shown in the *Traffic* exhibition, are exquisite mementoes of each artist's unique, distinctive mode of thought. More generally, objectivity was not the point: rather, rationality had to be shown to be crazy by being enacted literally; the Organization Man was nuts, viz. General Idea, *Pilot* (1977).

Let us return to *One and Three Chairs* and see whether it meets these deeper criteria—Kosuth's own—of what counts as conceptual. In the most immediate sense, it looks like a simple demonstration. Signified + signifier = sign. All there, all at once. A rose is a rose is a rose. But there are two signifiers, after all, which open up a space of ambiguity (which may be closed again when we read the work as an illustration of Plato's three stages of knowledge). The project becomes more interesting when we realize that other chairs could be used under the same title, and other objects—for example, a shovel, à la Duchamp's *In Advance of the Broken Arm*, an authorized replica of which is owned by Kosuth. The point is that *One and Three Chairs* is not a one-off, singular visual statement: it is an instantiation of a proposition that may be realized using any matching set of elements. Like many other works conceived at the time, it is an exemplification of an act of thought. Kosuth's *Art as Idea* series seems to be a set of tautological objects: actually, they are visual propositions about themselves as signifying instances, presented

Art & Language (Mel Ramsden, England, b. 1944) (estab. 1967), Secret Painting, *1967–68. Oil on canvas and photostat, painting: 79 × 79 cm; text: 65.5 × 65.5 cm, Art Gallery of New South Wales. Purchased 2003. Photo: AGNSW. © Art & Language / Mel Ramsden 30.2003.a-b.*

as Art (or Art as Idea as Idea)—on the post–Ad Reinhardt grounds that that is all that art, in conscience, at this time, can be.[14]

A step forward was to take stated propositions as thesaural, which opens out their closure, their two-way tautology, as Kosuth did when he placed thesaural categories in newspapers in his *Second Investigation* (1968–69). In a parallel way Mel Ramsden's *Secret Painting*, made in 1967–68 in London en route to New York, becomes a comment on the limits of painting as a practice. Such questioning could be consequential: it released artists elsewhere in the world to begin an interrogative practice. For example, Robert MacPherson in the 1970s in Brisbane deployed this strategy to appropriate ordinary language use—in his case, roadside signs. So did Greg Curnoe, in his banner paintings of the 1980s.

Propositionality—its apparently categorical force, but also its materiality and its provisionality—is what language-based conceptualism recurs to: it is its core, from which it opens out again. First this is under-

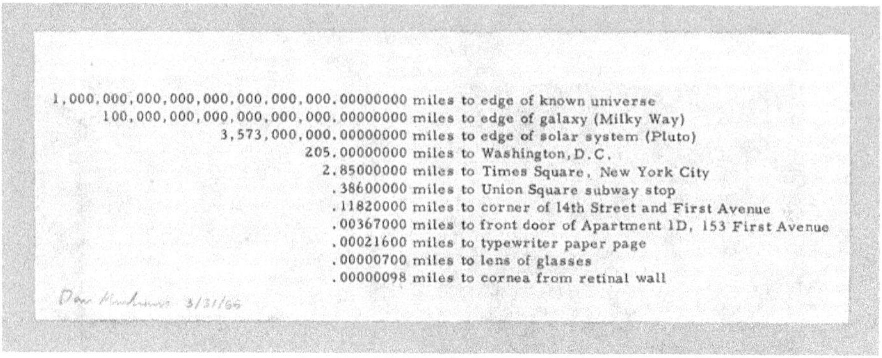

1,000,000,000,000,000,000,000,000.00000000 miles to edge of known universe
100,000,000,000,000,000,000.00000000 miles to edge of galaxy (Milky Way)
3,573,000,000.00000000 miles to edge of solar system (Pluto)
205.00000000 miles to Washington, D.C.
2.85000000 miles to Times Square, New York City
.38600000 miles to Union Square subway stop
.11820000 miles to corner of 14th Street and First Avenue
.00367000 miles to front door of Apartment 1D, 153 First Avenue
.00021600 miles to typewriter paper page
.00000700 miles to lens of glasses
.00000098 miles to cornea from retinal wall

Daniel ["Dan"] Graham, March 31, 1966, *1966. Typewriting on paper on board, 12 ¾ × 15 ¾ inches (32.4 × 40 cm). Partial gift of the Daled Collection and partial purchase through the generosity of Maja Oeri and Hans Bodenmann, Sue and Edgar Wachenheim III, Marlene Hess and James D. Zirin, Agnes Gund, Marie-Josee and Henry R. Kravis, and Jerry I. Speyer and Katherine G. Farley © The Museum of Modern Art, New York, NY, U.S.A./Licensed by SCALA/Art Resource, NY.*

stood spatially (sculpture is residual here), as in Dan Graham's *March 31, 1966*, a description that evokes a spatial zooming beyond spatiality. (His *Schema* for *Aspen* magazine, and for the first issue of *Art-Language*, is his masterwork). Then it is understood as a phenomenon of perception (painting is residual here), as in Ian Burn's *No object implies the existence of any other* (1967). This is, in fact, a thought that is impossible to have in a literal sense: you cannot think the idea of an object not implying another object without thinking about at least two objects, one and an other; in front of an object made to be seen by an other (us), consisting of a statement on a mirror that cannot but show you yourself and other objects. (That is, it demonstrates the rest of Hobbes's statement, ". . . that is, if we consider these objects in themselves and never look beyond the ideas that inform them.") Yoko Ono was closer to Hobbes in her 1961 "proposal": *Painting to Let the Evening Light Go Through*. Burn's *Xerox Book* (1968) is more resolute: it embodies the idea of a tautological process.

LeWitt's thirty-fifth and last sentence read: "These sentences comment on art, but are not art." The editorial to the first issue of *Art-Language*, in which these sentences appeared in 1969, asked itself the question, "What would follow [for the art community of language users] if this editorial itself came up for the count as a work of art?"

It is these innovations that allow us to recognize the second proposition in my theory of conceptualism:

> 2. That, as well as being a set of practices for interrogating what it was for perceiving subjects and perceived objects to be in the world (that is, it was an inquiry into the minimal situations in which art might be possible), conceptualism was also a further integrated set of practices for interrogating the conditions under which the first interrogation becomes possible and necessary (that is, an inquiry into the maximal conditions for art to be thought).

CONCEPTUAL ART ARRIVES

Conceptual Art arrives as a paradoxical supplement, and art-institutional instantiation, of the interaction between these two approaches. By 1970 we were well inside an art movement, as evidenced by the number of books, exhibitions, articles, and so forth, with Idea Art, Konzept Kunst, and so on, in their titles. This includes Lucy Lippard's exhibitions and the *Six Years* book, as well as exhibitions such as *45°30'N-73°36'W + Inventory*, presented in Montreal in 1971 by Gary Coward with Arthur Bardo and Bill Vazan.

Common consensus now is that the full-glare moment of art-world and public recognition was the 1970 exhibition *Conceptual Art and Conceptual Aspects*, curated by Donald Karshan at the New York Cultural Center (with Kosuth and Burn as "ghost curators"). Note that the double has already appeared: yes, there is core Conceptual Art, but there is also art that has some conceptual qualities ("aspects"), that is, there is also conceptual*ist* art.

But there was, by 1971, a big shift under way within the movement itself, leading to the third element of my theory:

> 3. The conditions—social, languaged, cultural, and political—of practices (1) and (2) were problematized, as was communicative exchange as such (that is, in-

> quiry became an active engagement in the pragmatic conditions that might generate a defeasible sociality).

Put more simply, if Art & Language's self-critique was at the core of conceptualism at this time (as in the indexing projects such as *Index 01*, 1972, at Documenta 5), other artists were taking up these analytical procedures and applying them to real-life situations. Obviously, this occurred differently in different places, and differently again for artists in transit between them. Well-known examples are Hans Haacke's *Shapolsky et al.* (1971) and Mary Kelly's *Post-Partum Document* (1973–79). Less known are Martha Wilson's *Chauvinistic Pieces*, 1971: these are an extraordinary application of nominative generalities to life situations so as to bring out the absurd gap between the two, and the power structures built into them. For instance, *Unknown Piece* has this instruction: "A woman is prevented from knowing the identity of her partner (sleeping pill, blindfold, total darkness) with certainty. On the evidence the child's features give her, she guesses who she slept with." *Determined Piece*: "A woman selects a couple for the genetic features she admires (good teeth, curly hair, green eyes, etc.) and raises their baby." *Chauvinistic Piece*: "A man is injected with the hormones that produce symptoms of motherhood." It is as if the 1960s, far from being the moment of free love and so forth, was already organized along the lines of Plato's *Republic*.[15]

Transformations occurred within Art & Language, such that its work joined the third sense I have identified. We realized that our extreme adoption of avant-garde strategies was belated, was infused with a sense that we were being avant-gardists after the death of the form. When Allan Kaprow invited me to lecture at CalArts in 1974, he introduced me as "a living dinosaur, an actual avant-gardist." Thus we moved to embed our practice in the world, starting with ourselves as actors in the art world.[16] *Blurting in A&L* (1973) enables readers to enter a conversation and shape it according to their own preferences; *Draft for an Anti-Textbook* was a 1974 issue of *Art-Language* that, among other things, took on provincialism in theory; the exhibitions recorded in *Art & Language Australia* (1975) did so in practice. The three issues of *The Fox* (1975–76) constitute the group's most direct assault on the modernist art world. Ian Burn, Nigel Lendon, and I continued this kind of work in Australia when we returned in the mid-1970s, creating an Art & Working Life movement that persists, in a dispersed fashion, to this day.[17] Karl Beveridge and Carole Condé's comic book *It's Still Privileged Art*

(1976) was based on Maoist practices of constant self-criticism; the Cultural Revolution comes to the New York art world (we saw a lot of these publications in Chinatown).[18] I cannot overstress how important critical conceptualism was for the success of work with trade unions and dissident groups in Australia, Toronto, and elsewhere, and how important this particular commitment to consequence remains for subsequent artists of major caliber (such as Jeff Wall and Allan Sekula), as well as for the hundreds of artist collectives that operate all over the world today with this kind of work as part of their inspirational armory.

CONCEPTUALISM ALREADY REDUX

Now we arrive at the moment *after* Conceptual Art, when "conceptualism" appeared as a term in art discourse. Let us examine it from the point of view of the "theory" I have advanced. The key question will be: are we looking at delayed, or belated, or simply particular, peculiar, and other instances of (1) and (2), a local instance of (3), or is this a fourth sense/term/proposition that must be added to the three so far advanced? My answer will be: yes, no, and yes. One and three ideas, non-contemporaneously and contemporaneously, again. I will explore two cases among the many that arose during these years all over the world.

When Boris Groys coined the term "Moscow Romantic Conceptualism" in 1979, he created a verbal artifact that, I believe, attempted to stand at the same kind of critical (ironic yet implicated) distance from international art discourse and to its own circumstances of production, as he understood the art itself to be. Writing for readers in Russia (knowing that the circulation of his essay there would be clandestine), and for readers in France, who would presumably read it in English, he wanted to draw attention to how deeply embedded this kind of work was in the specific conditions of what it was to make "apartment art" in Moscow, to the awkward, embattled, ironic inwardness of the work (the artists wished to be anywhere but Moscow, but could not be). Similarly, in a society that ignored or repressed them, and was condemned to the skeptical resignation that filled "the Russian soul" like a lead balloon, the artists could only dream of being regarded as paragons of heightened subjectivism like the German and English Romantics. But dream they did—and why not; dreams are cheap. Finally, their art stood at a deliberate distance from the concerns and character of U.S. and European Conceptual Art as we have discussed it. Thus, by "Conceptualism"

Groys meant that this art was *like* such art in its self-reflective character, but in reverse, precisely in its deliberate effort to be intuitive, allusive, affective—that is, nonconceptual. In other words, each term within Groys's label had its opposite built into it—thus its acuity, as an art critical artifact.

In the 1979 issue of *A-YA*, the English translation of Groys's essay had some oddities. It offers two definitions, the first of which states that "the word 'conceptualism' may be understood in the narrower sense as designating a specific artistic movement clearly limited to place, time and origin."[19] The revised translation in *History Becomes Form* adds the phrase "and limited to a specific number of practitioners" to this sentence.[20] The reference here is to U.S. and European Conceptual Art. The second definition is this:

> Or, it may be interpreted more broadly, by referring to any attempt to withdraw from considering art works as material objects intended for contemplation and aesthetic evaluation. Instead, it could encourage solicitation and formation of the conditions that determine the viewer's perception of the work of art, the process of its inception by the artist, its relation to factors in the environment, and its temporal status.[21]

The recent translation changes the last two ideas to "its positioning in a certain context, and its historical status." This ties the description more closely to the Moscow group, and to art concerned with art, but it remains rather general.

"Romantic" got dropped from the term in the years after 1989, when this art (as distinct from the modernist, informal, protest art) began to be read as a prefiguration of the collapse of the Soviet system, and as the basis for all subsequent art in Russia of any seriousness. Groys's pragmatism enables us to see other artists carrying on the spirit of the Moscow Romantic Conceptualists, albeit in equally unorthodox ways. His key exemplars are Andrei Monastyrsky and the Collective Actions group, which dedicated itself to actions that heightened the specificity of everyday life while remaining, at the same time, scarcely distinguishable from it. The Medical Hermeneutics group made "work" from speculation about whether such actions were art or life.

To me, the real parallels in work such as Ilya Kabakov's *Answers of the Experimental Group* (1971)—the originary moment of "Moscow Conceptualism," according to Matthew Jesse Jackson—are with the interrogatory nature of the late 1950s/early 1960s work of Johns, Rauschenberg, and Warhol, which I have suggested is conceptual in the broad sense of the term.[22] More precisely, it accords with my first proposition above, that conceptualism was, at its various beginnings, a set of practices for interrogating what it was for perceiving subjects and perceived objects to be in the world, and the minimal situations in which art might be possible. Moscow Conceptualism is not consonant with my second proposition, exemplified by the Adornoesque negative criticality of Kosuth et al., yet it is in quite specific ways an instance of the third. The fact that it was produced after the institutionalization of Conceptual Art means that one element in its makeup was a refusal of such art, a sense that adopting its modes would be irrelevant to local concerns and to local audiences. I do not see any artist working in the Soviet sphere as producing classical Conceptual Art—indeed, there is no reason to expect that anyone would wish to do so. On the other hand, groups such as Collective Actions and Medical Hermeneutics and a number of individual artists were, in the 1970s and 1980s, making art in a context where they were aware of Conceptual Art before and during Conceptual Art, and were contemporaries with conceptualist art after it, so they made their choices accordingly. Again, the work emerges out of the concerns expressed in my third proposition. If parallels have to be found, it is closest to Fluxus in Europe.

In his otherwise excellent survey, Jackson never questions the term "Moscow Conceptualism." There are, however, extensive discussions of it, along with a range of other terms that were in use at the time and that have been developed since, in the new book edited by Alla Rosenfeld, *Moscow Conceptualism in Context*.[23] The most detailed account is "The Banner without a Slogan: Definitions and Sources of Moscow Conceptualism" by Marek Bartelik, who concludes a useful survey by warning us against the danger of those who would manage the politics of memory:

> It is crucial, therefore, to assure that the history of the movement not be reduced to a few textbook names of artists at the expense of others who for some reason or another fell out of the picture. In other words, our history of Moscow Conceptualism should be inclusive rather than exclusive of as many artists as possible. After all, it was Moscow Conceptualism's ethereal, dispersed, and fragmentary nature—as opposed to the official, solid, and permanent nature of Socialist Realism

> and its correlates—that helped its development and survival for more than twenty years, and that constitutes its unique value for today's audiences in both Russia and the West.[24]

This is well meant, but it does not tackle the point about consequence. A similar politics of hope drove the curatorial project that has been most influential in defining the term "conceptualism" in art discourse in recent decades. In their foreword to *Global Conceptualism: Points of Origin, 1950s–1980s*, Luis Camnitzer, Jane Farver, and Rachel Weiss distinguish two periods, "two relatively distinct waves of activity": the late 1950s to around 1973, during which time worldwide political changes led artists to call into question the underlying ideas of art and its institutional systems, and the mid-1970s to the end of the 1980s, when artists mostly outside Euro-America abandoned formalist or traditional art practices for conceptualist art.[25] As they write:

> It is important to delineate a clear distinction between *conceptual art* as a term used to denote an essentially formalist practice developed in the wake of minimalism, and *conceptualism*, which broke decisively from the historical dependence of art upon physical form and its visual appreciation. Conceptualism was a broader attitudinal expression that summarized a wide array of works and practices which, in radically reducing the role of the art object, reimagined the possibilities of art vis-à-vis the social, political and economic realities within which it was being made. Its informality and affinity for collectivity made conceptualism attractive to those artists who yearned for a more direct engagement with the public during those intense, transformative periods. For them, the de-emphasis—or the dematerialization—of the object allowed the artistic energies to move from the object to the conduct of art.[26]

The implication is that Euro-American style Conceptual Art—even as it came to dominate understandings of what counted as Conceptual Art—amounted to little more than an essentially formalist critique of minimalism. It was an internal art-world style change, whereas conceptualist tendencies elsewhere were always broader, more social and political, and became more so as time went on, eventually eclipsing Euro-American tendencies. Works by Camnitzer, such as his *Uruguayan*

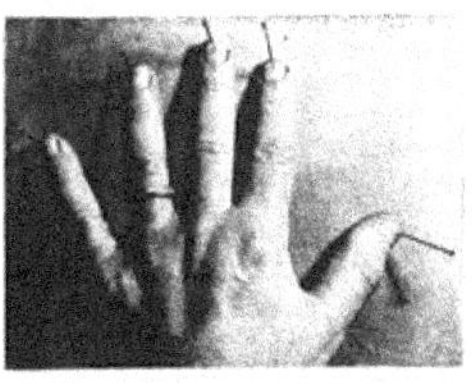

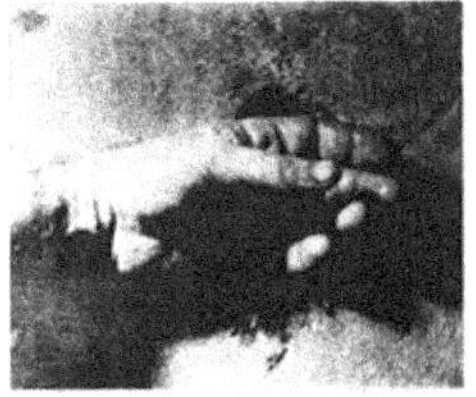

Left: *Luis Camnitzer,* He practiced every day, *plate 2 from* Uruguayan Torture Series, *1983–84. Photo etching 29.53 × 21.65 inches (75.01 × 54.99 cm). Courtesy Alexander Gray Associates, New York © 2015 Luis Camnitzer/Artists Rights Society (ARS), New York.*

Right: *Luis Camnitzer,* The sense of order was seeping away, *plate 31 from* Uruguayan Torture Series, *1983–84. Photo etching 29.53 × 21.65 inches (75.01 × 54.99 cm). Courtesy Alexander Gray Associates, New York © 2015 Luis Camnitzer/Artists Rights Society (ARS), New York.*

Torture Series (1983–84), give some substance to this view.[27] While in general I support this openness, especially as we come closer to the present, we must also be watchful that it does not lapse into a kind of reverse reductivism, one that downplays the internal complexities of Euro-American conceptualism and fails to see its progressive transformations, as suggested by my propositions.

The *Global Conceptualism* curators did espouse a critical geopolitics, noting that the changes within conceptualism occurred most significantly on local levels: "the reading of 'globalism' that informs this project is a highly differentiated one, in which localities are linked in crucial ways but not subsumed into a homogenized set of circumstances and responses to them. We mean to denote a multicentered map with various points of origin in which local events are crucial determinants."[28] A number of interesting alternative terms appear in the essays, including "Non-object art," applied to Hélio Oiticica's *parangolés* by Brazilian critic Ferreira Gullar in 1959, and "Post-Object Art," used by aesthetician and sculptor Donald Brook in Sydney in 1968–69. Curators from all over the world were invited to mount mini-exhibitions of art that would meet this understanding of conceptualism. Margarita Tupitsyn argued that in Russia two tendencies—Kabakovian "stylelessness" and Sots Art (Soviet kitsch into high art)—combined to generate a word-image interplay that was uniquely inflected by its peculiarly Soviet context.[29]

In some of these situations, it may be that "conceptualism" works as a substitute for what I believe the artists involved were—and remain—primarily concerned about: as Reiko Tomii demonstrates in the case of Japan, they sought recognition of their contemporaneity with the Euro-American artists, and even of their precedence in some cases.[30] Given that Conceptual Art was the most radical, avant-garde, innovative, and consequential-seeming art of the time and has retained much of that aura since, they wanted to expand its definition to include themselves. On the most obvious level of simple fairness, they want to be seen to have been contemporary. This, I suggest, is actually more important to many of those involved than whether or not their art was, or may now be seen to be, conceptual.

From the perspective of the broad historical account that I am developing in my work at the moment, I see these artists as wishing to be acknowledged as equally important innovators within the worldwide shift from late modern to contemporary art.[31] In this sense, they are right to seek such acknowledgment. However, like all claims for consequence, it comes with responsibilities.

CONTEMPORANEITY

Mel Ramsden described Conceptual Art as "like Modernism's nervous breakdown."[32] A more parochial way of putting it was "Clement Greenberg's nightmare" (although that had already happened, in 1959, when Frank Stella made his black paintings, and MoMA exhibited them). Michael Fried's nightmare, then. From my perspective, these intense disputations are all indicative of the moment in which late modern art became contemporary, that is, it was obliged to change fundamentally as part of the general transformation of modernity into our current con-

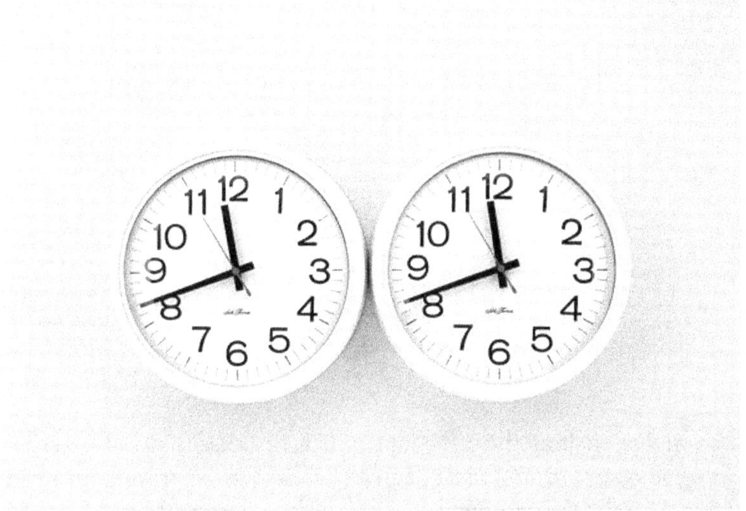

Felix Gonzalez-Torres, "Untitled" (Perfect Lovers), *1991.*
Clocks, paint on wall, overall 14 × 28 × 2 ¾ inches (35.6 × 71.2 × 7 cm).
Gift of the Dannheisser Foundation © The Museum of Modern Art / Licensed by SCALA / Art Resource, NY.

dition, in which the contemporaneity of difference, not our declining modernity or passé postmodernity, is definitive of experience.

Clearly, there is a spirit of openhandedness in post–Conceptual Art uses of the term "Conceptualism." We can now endow it with a capital letter because it has grown in scale from its initial designation of an avant-garde grouping, or various groups in various places, and has evolved in two further phases. It became something like a movement, on par with and evolving at the same time as Minimalism. Thus the sense it has in a book such as Tony Godfrey's *Conceptual Art*.[33] Beyond that, it has in recent years spread to become a tendency, a resonance within art practice that is nearly ubiquitous. Thus the widespread use of terms such as "post-conceptual" as a prefix to painting such as that of Gerhard Richter and photography such as that of Andreas Gursky. And the appeal for inclusiveness cited earlier, as well as the nearly universal use of "conceptual" for any art based on any kind of idea (as distinct from it issuing from instinct, taste, or the materials).

But inclusiveness, however desirable, does not mean that everyone

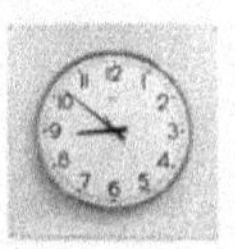

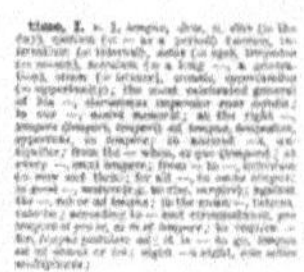
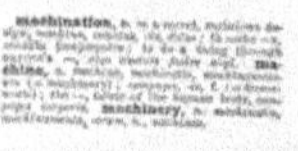
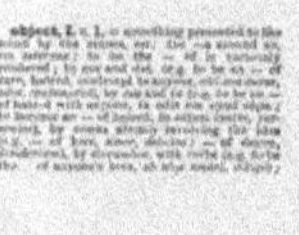

Joseph Kosuth, Clock (One and Five), *1965. Clock and four works on paper, photograph, and printed paper. Tate Modern, London. Acquisition transferred from the Irish Museum of Modern Art 1997 © Tate, London 2015.*

was, and is, making the same kind of art, nor that they did so, or are doing so now, with the same degree of consequence. If we want to address critically the contemporary ubiquity of the idea that "after Conceptual art, all art is conceptual" (of course echoing Kosuth on Duchamp in 1969, but in a bland, generalizing fashion), we could do worse than contrast a piece by Kosuth, *Clock (One and Five)* (1965) (in the Tate collection, London), with a celebrated work by Felix Gonzalez-Torres, *"Untitled" (Perfect Lovers)* (1991). We can see in retrospect that Kosuth is searching for his "Art as Idea" format; he had not quite settled on the absolute tautology that drives it in the classic three-part presentations with which we are familiar. Instead, he lines up a photograph, an object, and a set of definitions that display the conceptual architecture of clock-time, arraying it across its pictorial, mechanical, and linguistic aspects. One thing after another, Judd-like, in a row, minimally. Five ways of shaping time are displayed. The printed definition of "time" is front and center and is flanked on one side by an actual clock ticking time along and away, and by a photograph that will forever freeze the time shown on the clock it recorded but which will, being printed on paper, itself fade. On the other side are printed definitions of "mechanization" and of "object," concepts that elaborate the contexts of both the clock and the camera. The idea world of clock-time is being probed, its relevant concepts being assembled almost spatially. This is conceptualism just before it becomes Conceptual Art, the quest before the rigor sets in.

If, in regard to Pop art and Euro-American conceptualism, we are, as Boris Groys has remarked, looking at art that presumes a society built on freedom of choice (however apparent, spectacularized, and ultimately consumerist it may be), for the Moscow Romantic Conceptualists the very idea of having a choice was but a dream (yet impossibility is precisely what occasions dreams). This, too, but very differently, is the point of *"Untitled" (Perfect Lovers)*. The only "choice" for lovers in a time of AIDS was about the manner in which they died—including whether they died together, as comrades of a dying time.

Consequence counts differently at different times, in different places. This, above all, is what we need to keep in mind when we puzzle over what was at stake in art when it was made, and what we need to look for in art that is being made now.

NOTES

This chapter was originally published as Terry Smith, "One and Three Ideas: Conceptualism Before, During, and After Conceptual Art," e-flux journal 29 *(November 2011), http://www.e-flux.com/journal/view/267, and was subsequently reprinted in Boris Groys, ed.,* Moscow Symposium: Conceptualism Revisited *(Berlin: Sternberg, 2012), 42–72.*

The remarks in this chapter combine elements from three lectures. The first was delivered on November 27, 2010, at a conference organized by Barbara Fischer, director of the Justina M. Barnicke Gallery, University of Toronto, in association with the exhibition Traffic: Conceptualism in Canada, *shown at the University of Toronto Galleries during the preceding months. The second, dedicated to the memory of Charles Harrison, was delivered at the Courtauld Institute of Art, University of London, on March 8, 2011, as part of a series on Global Conceptualism organized by Sarah Wilson and Boris Groys. The third was presented on April 14, 2011, as part of a conference titled "Revisiting Conceptual Art: The Russian Case in an International Context," convened by Boris Groys and organized by the Stella Art Foundation, Moscow. I would like to thank all those concerned.*

Epigraph: Cited on a file card from the catalog/exhibition by Gary Coward with Arthur Bardo and Bill Vazan, 45°30'N-73°36'W + Inventory, *Williams Art Gallery, Montreal, 1971.*

1. Simon Blackburn, *The Oxford Dictionary of Philosophy* (Oxford: Oxford University Press, 1994), s.v. "conceptualism."

2. Terry Smith, "Peripheries in Motion: Conceptualism and Conceptual Art in Australia and New Zealand," in Luis Camnitzer, Jane Farver, and Rachel Weiss, eds., *Global Conceptualism: Points of Origin, 1950s–1980s* (New York: Queens Museum of Art, 1999), 87–95.

3. Ian Burn, "Conceptual Art as Art," *Art and Australia* (September 1970): 167–70.

4. During the 1990s, Burn became acutely aware of what he saw as the growing disjunction between the histories of art written by art historians and what he saw as the historical work, on both art and history, being undertaken in certain works of art: "While any image or object can be fitted into many historical discourses, it cannot be at the expense of the historical discourse within the image itself." Ian Burn, "Is Art History Any Use to Artists?," in *Dialogue: Writings in Art History* (Sydney: Allen and Unwin, 1991), 6. To Burn, artists created that discourse less as picturing of it (as if it were a parade occurring at a representable distance), more in the way they composed their works, in the disposition of elements internal to each work. Sidney Nolan and Fernand Léger were prominent examples: in one of his essays, Burn showed that Nolan used some compositional ideas of Léger's not to create a local modernism, nor to modernize his own art by imitation, but to negotiate a reconception of what landscape might mean in Australian art and history. See "Sidney Nolan: Landscape and Modern Life," in Burn, *Dialogue*, 67–85.

5. Conversation with Joseph Kosuth, New York, March 27, 2011.

6. An observation made by Boris Groys in a seminar at the Courtauld Institute, University of London, March 9, 2011.

7. "Before the Warhol canvases we are trapped in ghastly embarrassment. This sense of arbitrary coloring, the nearly obliterated image and the persistently intrusive feeling. Somewhere in the image there is a proposition. It is unclear." David Antin, "Warhol: The Silver Tenement," *Art News* (Summer 1966): 58.

8. I first published these propositions, under the heading "A Theory of Conceptualism," in "Conceptual Art in Transit," chapter 6 of *Transformations in Australian Art, vol. 2: The Twentieth Century—Modernism and Aboriginality* (Sydney: Craftsman House, 2002), 127. They may be found in a nascent form, but applied to the Art & Language group only, in my essay "Art and Art and Language," *Artforum* (February 1974): 49–52.

9. "'Concept Art' is first of all an art of which the material is concepts, as the material of, e.g., music is sound. Since concepts are closely bound up with language, concept art is the kind of art of which the material is language." Henry Flynt, "Concept Art," in La Monte Young, ed., *An Anthology* (New York: George Maciunas and Jackson MacLow, 1962).

10. Morris is just one among many artists whose breakthrough work during the 1960s and 1970s has led to a practice that is at once innovative, reactive to the innovations of younger artists, and retrospective with respect to itself and the innovations of contemporaries past and present. This is a (remodernist) resonance within contemporary art that calls for careful analysis and cautious synopsis.

11. "For the artist . . . is concerned only with the way (1) in which art is

capable of conceptual growth and (2) how his propositions are logically capable of following that growth." Joseph Kosuth, "Art after Philosophy," *Studio International* 178, nos. 915–17 (1969); in Joseph Kosuth, *Art after Philosophy and After: Collected Writings, 1966–1990* (Cambridge, MA: MIT Press, 1991), 20. It is interesting that his illustrations of such propositions include this: "If Pollock is important it is because he painted on loose canvas horizontally to the floor," not because he hung them on the wall subsequently, and even less due to his notions of "self-expression" (21). Robert Bailey has said in conversation that Kosuth's statement could also be taken to mean that after Duchamp drew attention to the conceptual core of consequential art, all art of consequence made at any time anywhere is ipso facto conceptual. This is an idea that unleashes a quest of reinterpretation of potentially immense proportions.

12. Sol LeWitt, "Paragraphs on Conceptual Art," *Artforum* (Summer 1967): 79–83.

13. Sol LeWitt, "Sentences on Conceptual Art," *Art-Language* 1, no. 1 (May 1969): 11–13. Five versions in manuscript are reproduced in Suzanne Héman, Jurie Poot, and Hripsimé Visser, eds., *Conceptual Art in the Netherlands and Belgium 1965–1975* (Rotterdam: NAi Publishers for the Stedelijk Museum Amsterdam), 48–83.

14. Among Canadian artists working in New York at the time, Michael Snow's *Authorization* (1969) gets close to this, but the mirror makes it not tautological: it is at least partly about not being able to see one's whole reflection and is thus partly consonant with Warhol's filmmaking. Nor should we forget the obvious fact that it is also a real metaphor for the process of being "authorized"—recorded by authority, as in having a passport photograph taken. Snow's work *Red to the Fifth* is tautological: it is a demonstration piece that leaves nothing dangling—rare in Snow's art, to my knowledge.

15. A similar set of instructions with slightly different wording is cited in Lucy R. Lippard, *Six Years: The Dematerialization of the Art Object from 1966 to 1972* (New York: Praeger, 1973), 227.

16. See Smith, "Art and Art and Language."

17. See Sandy Kirby, ed., *Ian Burn, Art: Critical, Political* (Nepean, Australia: University of Western Sydney, 1996).

18. See Bruce Barber, ed., *Condé and Beveridge: Class Works* (Halifax, Nova Scotia: The Press of the Nova Scotia College of Art and Design, 2008).

19. Boris Groys, "Moscow Romantic Conceptualism," *A-YA* 1 (1979): 1.

20. Boris Groys, *History Becomes Form: Moscow Conceptualism* (Cambridge, MA: MIT Press, 2010), 35.

21. Groys, "Moscow Romantic Conceptualism," 1.

22. Matthew Jesse Jackson, *The Experimental Group: Ilya Kabakov, Moscow Conceptualism, Soviet Avant-Gardes* (Chicago: University of Chicago Press, 2010), 110.

23. Alla Rosenfeld, *Moscow Conceptualism in Context* (Munich: Prestel for the Zimmerli Art Museum at Rutgers University, 2011).

24. Marek Bartelik, "The Banner without a Slogan: Definitions and Sources of Moscow Conceptualism," in Rosenfeld, *Moscow Conceptualism in Context*, 16.

25. Luis Camnitzer, Jane Farver, and Rachel Weiss, "Foreword," in Camnitzer, Farver, and Weiss, *Global Conceptualism*, vii.

26. Camnitzer, Farver, and Weiss, "Foreword," viii.

27. The Museo del Barrio show could have done better in this regard, but the catalog is comprehensive. See Hans-Michael Herzog and Katrin Steffen, *Luis Camnitzer* (Ostfildern, Germany: Hatje-Cantz for Daros Museum, Zurich, 2010).

28. Camnitzer, Farver, and Weiss, "Foreword," vii.

29. Margarita Tupitsyn, "About Early Soviet Conceptualism," in Camnitzer, Farver, and Weiss, *Global Conceptualism*, 98–107.

30. Reiko Tomii, "Historicizing 'Contemporary Art': Some Discursive Practices in Gendai Bijutsu in Japan," *positions* 12, no. 3 (2004): 611–41.

31. See Terry Smith, *Contemporary Art: World Currents* (London: Laurence King, 2011).

32. Cited in Charles Harrison, *Conceptual Art and Painting: Further Essays on Art & Language* (Cambridge, MA: MIT Press, 2001), 27.

33. Tony Godfrey, *Conceptual Art* (London: Phaidon, 1998). The most comprehensive compendium, unmatched in its coverage of Central and Eastern European work in particular but global in its reach, is Miško Šuvaković, *Konceptualna Umetnost* (Novi Sad, Serbia: Muzej Savremene Umetnosti Vojvodine, 2007).

Index

Note: Page numbers in *italics* indicate illustrations.

www.ingramcontent.com/pod-product-compliance
Lightning Source LLC
LaVergne TN
LVHW020510100826
845148LV00003B/741

9780822361312